# BRISTOL BAY BASIN

Volume 5, Number 3, 1978

**ALASKA GEOGRAPHIC**

# The Alaska Geographic Society

*To teach many more to better know and use our natural resources*

**About This Issue:** BRISTOL BAY BASIN has evolved over the past several years, getting its start in 1974 when Lael Morgan, associate editor of **ALASKA**® magazine, was assigned to spend time in the area assessing the impact of the 1973 fishing season, one of the worst on record. A veteran reporter familiar to many readers, Lael has worked for several newspapers, both in and out of Alaska, and has been associated with Alaska Northwest Publishing Company since early 1974. She has filed stories on life in bush villages, the effects of the Alaska Native Claims Settlement Act, Eskimo whaling, several Alaskan artists, and is the author of three books. Lael supplied most of the text for this edition, and many of the photographs (photos lacking specific credit are hers).

Special thanks to several Bristol Bay residents and others knowledgeable on the subject for their information and help in reviewing the text—Chuck and Sara Hornberger of Lake Clark; George Johanson, veteran Bristol Bay fisherman; Ole Mathisen and Pat Poe of the Fisheries Research Institute, University of Washington College of Fisheries; Jim Dodson of the Alaska Air Carriers Association; Laurence Freeburn, long-time canneryman; and Neil Johannsen of the Alaska Division of Parks. Thanks also to the many Bristol Bay residents who contributed photographs and a wealth of information on the Bay.

**Editors:** Robert A. Henning, Marty Loken, Barbara Olds, Lael Morgan.
**Associate Editor:** Penny Rennick
**Editorial Assistance:** Jim Rearden, Robert N. De Armond, Tim Jones, Betty Johannsen
**Designer:** Roselyn Pape
**Cartographer:** Jon.Hersh

THE ALASKA GEOGRAPHIC SOCIETY is a nonprofit organization exploring new frontiers of knowledge across the lands of the polar rim, learning how other men and other countries live in their Norths, putting the geography book back in the classroom, exploring new methods of teaching and learning—sharing in the excitement of discovery in man's wonderful new world north of 51°16'.

MEMBERS OF THE SOCIETY RECEIVE *Alaska Geographic*®, a quality magazine in color which devotes each quarterly issue to monographic in-depth coverage of a northern geographic region or resource-oriented subject.

MEMBERSHIP DUES in The Alaska Geographic Society are $20 for initiation and the first year, $16 thereafter. (Eighty percent of the first year's dues is for a one-year subscription to *Alaska Geographic*®.) Order from The Alaska Geographic Society, Box 4-EEE, Anchorage, Alaska 99509; (907) 243-1484.

MATERIAL SOUGHT: The editors of *Alaska Geographic*® seek a wide variety of informative material on the lands north of 51°16' on geographic subjects—anything to do with resources and their uses (with heavy emphasis on quality color photography)—from Alaska, Northern Canada, Siberia, Japan—all geographic areas that have a relationship to Alaska in a physical or economic sense. (In mid-1978 editors were seeking photographs and other materials on the following subjects: Stikine River drainage; Yukon-Kuskokwim Delta region; shellfish and shellfisheries of Alaska; Aleutian Islands; Yukon River and its tributaries; Wrangell and Saint Elias Mountains; and Alaska's Great Interior.) We do not want material done in excessive scientific terminology. A query to the editors is suggested. Payments are made for all material upon publication.

CHANGE OF ADDRESS: The post office does not automatically forward *Alaska Geographic*® when you move. To insure continuous service, notify us six weeks before moving. Send us your new address and zip code (and moving date), your old address and zip code, and if possible send a mailing label from a copy of *Alaska Geographic*®. Send this information to *Alaska Geographic*® Mailing Offices, 130 Second Avenue South, Edmonds, Washington 98020.

Second-class postage paid at Edmonds, Washington 98020. Printed in U.S.A.

Registered Trademark: *Alaska Geographic*. Library of Congress catalog card number 72-92087.
ISSN 0361-1353; key title *Alaska Geographic*.
ISBN 0-88240-113-0

*Cover*—Sockeye salmon, lifeblood of the Bristol Bay economy, nearly fill a small creek during spawning season. (Rollie Ostermick)
*Contents page*—A Bristol Bay fisherman rows out to his gill-netter at dawn. (J. Scott Carter)
*Left*—Bristol Bay gill-netters await the next opening. (J. Scott Carter)

**T**o a somewhat greater degree than many of the various geographical areas of Alaska, Bristol Bay is a world unto itself, a transition zone between mountains and tundra, physically walled off by distance and terrain from the main body of Central Alaska, a great long boat voyage from shipping centers, and at the outer ends of the Alaskan airplane network.

Even the Russians did little here (the big early Russian centers of activity were at Kodiak and Sitka and Unalaska, all far away) and until the Second World War, Aleuts, and Eskimos, and Indians, all meeting and intermingling to various degrees here, along with a scattering of white fishermen, traders, trappers and occasional prospectors, lived a subsistence existence.

In the short frenzy from mid-June through July the old Bristol Bay sailboat gill-netters braved rough seas and miserable winds to reap sometimes great bonanzas of sockeye salmon—the greatest run of sockeyes in the world—and then, when the card games and the drinking and socializing of late summer had ended, the few men and their families who did not take the southbound boats, carefully outfitted for the long winters. Some

*Left*—Sockeye salmon crowd a stream in the Bristol Bay region during their summertime rush to spawning grounds. The region's sockeyes have been the mainstay of Bristol Bay's economy since the late 1800's. (Rollie Ostermick) *Below*—Double-ended Bristol Bay gill-netters sail across the Bay shortly before the demise of the sailboat fishery in 1951, when the use of powerboats was allowed. The sailboats always carried a crew of two, and required considerably more skill to operate than today's fast and more comfortable rigs. Many boats and men were lost and,

according to one veteran Scandinavian fisherman, "it was the toughest fishery in Alaska . . . next to fishing alone for halibut in an open dory." (U.W. Fisheries Research Institute)

5

The mud of the Bay,
a blue-gray gluey mess that
swallows hip boots,
is a thing no beach fisherman
will ever forget . . .

toughed it out on the nearby beaches. Many went "upriver" to hundreds of traplines and scattered Native villages and winter camps. They took foxes, a few mink and wolverine, otter, a few ermine and muskrat, now and then a wolf. In the spring they trapped beaver, the big cash crop . . . a ten-skin limit to everybody in the family, perhaps the first of the family welfare benefits to derive from government regulation. An extra child was an extra dollar.

It was a tough life—rugged people in a harsh, great rolling place of tundra with meandering, salmon-swollen rivers, snowy crags rimming the land to the far north and east, a smoking line of restless volcanoes receding southward into the mists. The mud of the Bay, a blue-gray gluey mess that swallows hip boots, is a thing no beach fisherman will ever forget. And the vastness of the never-ending sea of tundra between the northern mountains and the volcanoes to the south is accentuated by the almost-ceaseless wind. In the Iliamna country the Nondalton Indians used to say that when you saw the tall clumps of grass bouncing this way and that as the wind blew, creating an endless swaying, "That's the Moose Men going through." There must be an awful lot of Moose Men.

Low tide at an old cannery near the Nushagak River. (J. Scott Carter)

The Ahklun Mountains, sweeping northeast from Cape Newenham to form the northern edge of the Bristol Bay region, include many dramatic peaks. This view is in the Tikchik Lakes region. (Neil and Betty Johannsen)

Now there are airports where there used to be only river bars. A lot of snowmobiles and a smaller number of dog teams. And while there are highways in the planning stage, there also are plans to keep much of the land wild. And there are arguments about all plans to develop or preserve.

But the wind still blows in a big land with horizons far apart. Men still fish and salmon is still the big payday. There were the few Russians, the few traders and prospectors, the scattered soldier camps, the many canneries—and now, some sort of a not-yet-defined "Tomorrow" that may focus on oil, or parks, or a continuing increase in social welfare. It's hard to say. This is a rugged land of wind, fish, and vast distances, but change is a powerful thing. . . .

Robert A. Henning, President
The Alaska Geographic Society

# We could have told you, until recently, that this is one of the only places in America where a person can still live comfortably off the land . . .

Tom Klein hoists the hindquarter of a moose into a cache near a wilderness cabin in the eastern part of the Bristol Bay region. Overhunting has reduced moose and caribou numbers in recent years. "The days when people could live off the land are ended," said one resident, blaming guides, trophy hunters, "the people who fly out from Anchorage and the Kenai Peninsula, and the local people who chase the game on snow machines. . . ." (Rollie Ostermick)

# Introduction

# Bristol Bay: A Contradiction

The Bristol Bay region sits with its mountain-ridged back to the rest of the state; a continuing contradiction. Its coasts and waters were among the first to be exploited by Outsiders, while its interior rivers and lakes are still little known to many Alaskans.

This, at first glance, is deceptively tame country, spared the extremes of climate that make the Arctic so formidable. It has few record-high peaks to be conquered or the rocky reefs and narrows which often make Southeastern waters treacherous. Yet it is common for men to simply disappear here. Wrecked planes dot the landscape with unnerving predictability and the deep, cold waters seldom give up their dead.

Bristol Bay remains one of the most sparsely settled areas of Alaska— perhaps that's why those who live here are uniquely independent and unflappable. Anything that can't be cured with the application of a little Bag Balm or a .30-06 will probably take care of itself, they figure.

The land itself runs the gamut: lush, deep forests; sweeping, open tundra; many-faceted mountains; fickle passes; the largest and deepest of lakes; and rolling rivers of stunning beauty.

This is the home of the largest land carnivore (the Alaska brown bear) and smallest mammal (the shrew). It is here the birds choose to mass in the spring and fall. And here the world's most spectacular sockeye salmon runs come to spawn.

The charm of Bristol Bay had—at least until recent years—been one of the best-kept secrets in the state. A few years ago we could have safely stated that

"Bristol Bay is a place where people still do not lock their doors" . . . but that is becoming more difficult to say. We could have described the wild and wonderous animals we had seen—but many of them (especially moose and caribou) have been thinned out considerably by overhunting and other factors. We also could have told you, until recently, that "this is one of the only places in America where a person still can live comfortably off the land," but those days are numbered . . . or gone.

So we will tell you no more, in the hope that Bristol Bay's secret places will retain their value. The Bay has long been a mystery place, and deserves to hold on to at least some of its intrigue. . . .

*Lael Morgan*

*Lael Morgan, Associate Editor*
*ALASKA® magazine*

*Left*—Mama and two yearling brown bear cubs. The mother is watching another bear along a Bristol Bay region stream, while the youngsters look at the photographer. (Rollie Ostermick) *Right*—A crew from the University of Washington's Fisheries Research Institute, which has been conducting studies for years in the Bristol Bay region, leaves their Lake Nerka camp to net sticklebacks, young char and salmon smolt, which rise to the surface at night to feed on plankton. Lake Nerka, 36 miles long, is 30 miles north of Dillingham in the Wood River Lakes system. (Glen McDevitt)

**B**etween foothills are narrow, usually U-shaped valleys with glacial lakes sometimes 900 feet deep, cradled in bedrock

Mountains along the Alaska Peninsula, near Aniakchak Crater, east of Port Heiden. (Neil and Betty Johannsen)

12

# A Rugged Setting

Bristol Bay, the first big indentation of the Alaska coast north of the Alaska Peninsula, spans some 200 miles from its base at Port Moller to its northwest boundary at Cape Newenham and recedes northeastward almost the same distance to the mouths of the Nushagak and Kvichak rivers, which enrich its innermost reaches.

This watery province is comparatively shallow, with its deepest sounding only about 25 fathoms; yet since the beginning of history people have lived richly off the Bay's fish and sea mammals—Bristol Bay, in fact, has during its better seasons provided over 55% of the sockeye salmon consumed by our nation and 16% of the entire world catch.

The land mass of this region includes about 600 miles of shoreline and a small number of islands and islets as well as a lake-studded interior country, which is an integral part of the Bay by virtue of linking rivers, and because the whole is segregated from the rest of the state by imposing mountains.

The Bay's northern shore is guarded by a scattering of islands, the largest being Hagemeister, which is 24 miles long and reaches a height of 1,783 feet. The coastline here alternates between lovely hills and wooded country—Kulukak Bay for example—and low, flat tundra such as is found along the Togiak River. To the west, Jagged Mountain rises 2,350 feet just behind the apron of Cape Newenham, backed by sister peaks of the Ahklun Mountains. This steep-walled, craggy range is of heavily glaciated and deformed sedentary and volcanic origin from the late Paleozoic and early Mesozoic ages.

From western elevations of 1,000 to 2,000 feet, the Ahkluns become progressively rougher, reaching altitudes of more than 5,000 feet (Mount Oratia and Mount Waskey) in the northeast. Between foothills are narrow, usually U-shaped valleys with glacial lakes sometimes 900 feet deep, cradled in bedrock.

Hundreds of glass floats are scatterd along the outer beach of Nelson Lagoon, 20 miles west of Port Moller on the Alaska Peninsula. Port Moller marks the southwesternmost corner of the Bristol Bay region. (J. Nelson)

Southeast of the Ahkluns are the handsome Wood River Mountains, ranging from 2,000 to 3,500 feet and backing four interconnected lakes that tumble with sparkling clarity into Wood River and on to the Bay. North lie the rugged highlands of the Tikchik Mountains, once the site of extensive Pleistocene ice fields, now host to rock-lined glacial lakes of seemingly infinite number.

Continuing southeast, the interior heart of the region moderates to the rounded, rolling Nushagak Hills, then flattens into two major basins: the drainage of the great Nushagak River with its major tributary, the Mulchatna; and the shorter, swifter Kvichak, which carries the waters of Lake Clark and Iliamna Lake to the sea. The rivers form two bays deep within Bristol Bay, and break an otherwise uninterrupted shore. The land, which is moderately timbered in the north, levels here to a generally flat, pond-pocked, treeless tundra fronted by coastal flats of ever-shifting dark and pearl gray silt.

The southern reaches of the Bay along the Alaska Peninsula are more of the

*Opposite page*—Aerial view of the Bay of Islands, Iliamna Lake. The lake is the largest in Alaska with 1,000 square miles—see map on pages 16 and 17. (Neil and Betty Johannsen)
*Left*—Kijik Lake, near Lake Clark, an important salmon-spawning area. See map of Lake Clark on page 18. (Steve Behnke)
*Below*—A kayaker

crosses Lake Nerka, in the Wood River Lakes system. Recreational use of the Bristol Bay region has increased dramatically in recent years. (Neil and Betty Johannsen)

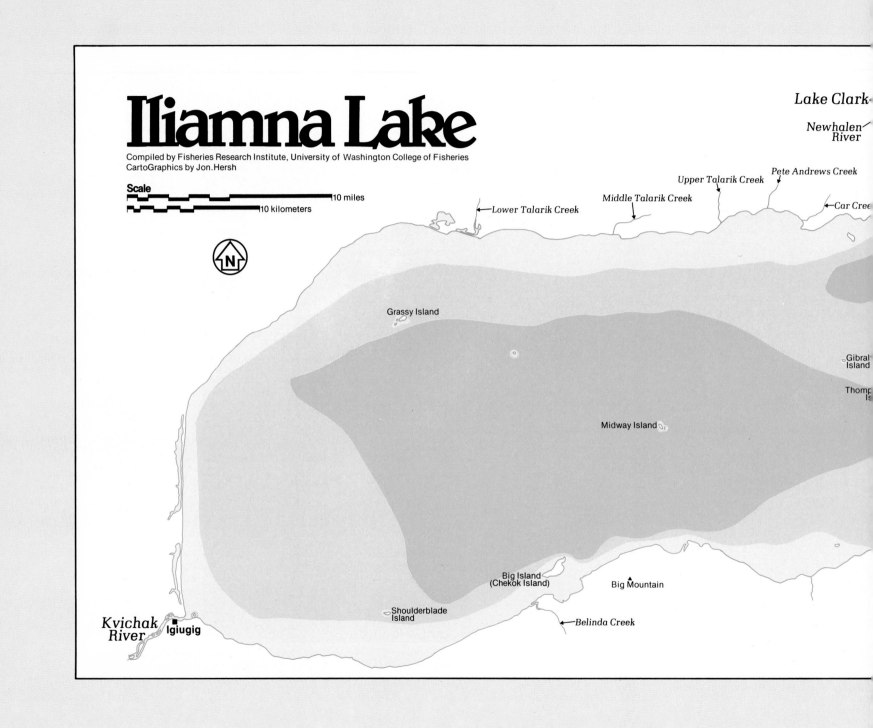

# Iliamna Lake

Compiled by Fisheries Research Institute, University of Washington College of Fisheries
CartoGraphics by Jon.Hersh

**Scale**

10 miles

10 kilometers

N

*Lake Clark*

*Newhalen River*

*Pete Andrews Creek*

*Upper Talarik Creek*

*Middle Talarik Creek*

← *Lower Talarik Creek*

← *Car Cree*

Grassy Island

Gibral Island

Thomp Is

Midway Island

Big Island (Chekok Island)

▲ Big Mountain

Shoulderblade Island

*Kvichak River*  ■ Igiugig

← *Belinda Creek*

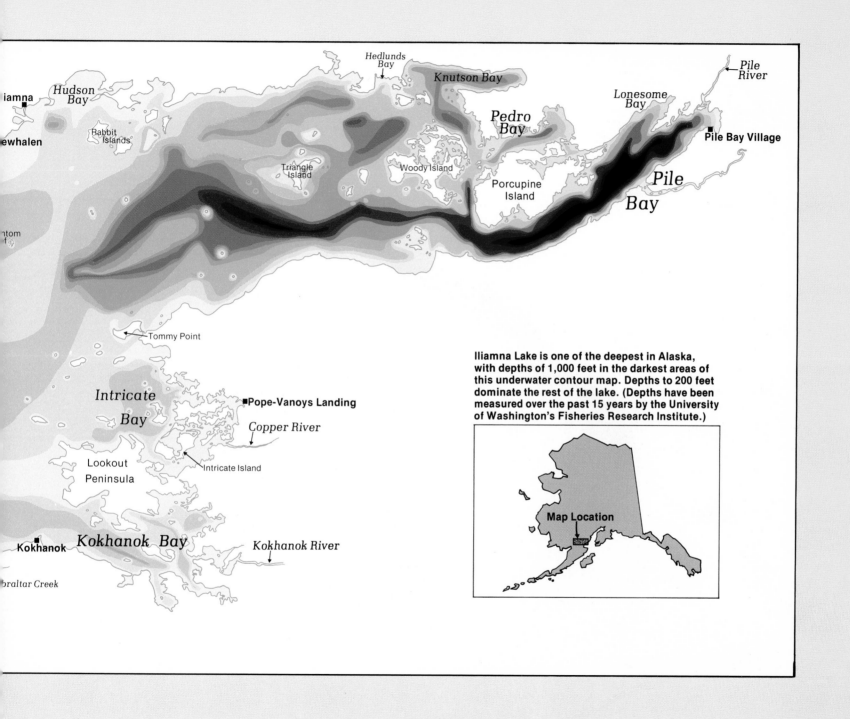

Hedlunds
Bay

Knutson Bay

Pile
River

liamna

Hudson
Bay

Lonesome
Bay

Rabbit
Islands

Pedro
Bay

Pile Bay Village

ewhalen

Triangle
Island

Woody Island

Pile
Bay

ntom
f

Porcupine
Island

Tommy Point

Iliamna Lake is one of the deepest in Alaska, with depths of 1,000 feet in the darkest areas of this underwater contour map. Depths to 200 feet dominate the rest of the lake. (Depths have been measured over the past 15 years by the University of Washington's Fisheries Research Institute.)

Intricate

Bay

■Pope-Vanoys Landing

Copper River

Lookout
Peninsula

Intricate Island

Map Location

Kokhanok Bay

Kokhanok River

Kokhanok

braltar Creek

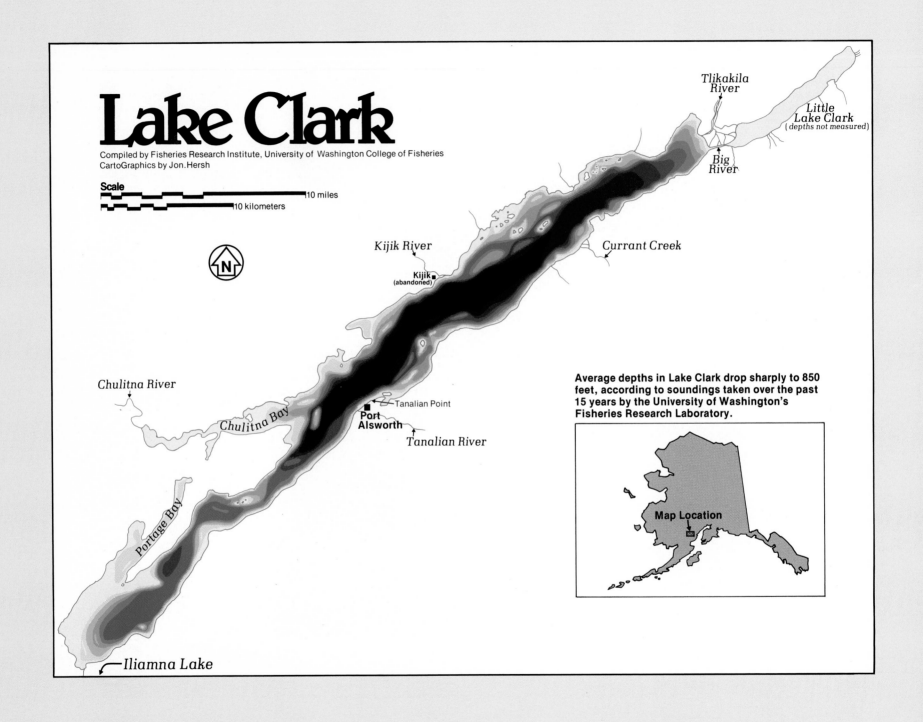

# Lake Clark

Compiled by Fisheries Research Institute, University of Washington College of Fisheries
CartoGraphics by Jon.Hersh

**Scale**

10 miles

10 kilometers

N

Tlikakila
River

Little
Lake Clark
(depths not measured)

Big
River

Kijik River

Currant Creek

Kijik
(abandoned)

Chulitna River

Chulitna Bay

Tanalian Point

Port
Alsworth

Tanalian River

Average depths in Lake Clark drop sharply to 850
feet, according to soundings taken over the past
15 years by the University of Washington's
Fisheries Research Laboratory.

Map Location

Portage Bay

Iliamna Lake

same—flat tundra with occasional moderate cliffs broken only by the King Salmon River, the Egegik River, which drains Becharof Lake; the mouth of the winding Ugashik farther to the southwest, and the notch that is Port Heiden at the mouth of the Meshik River. At the southernmost corner of the region, branching off Port Moller, Herendeen Bay makes a deep bite into the peninsula's mountain-ribbed back, giving mariners a glimpse of the awesome barrier that separates Bristol Bay from the Pacific Ocean.

This formidable boundary, the Aleutian Range, begins northeast of Bristol Bay's great lakes—Iliamna and Clark—where the majestic Alaska Range merges imperceptibly with a fiery string of volcanoes and is edged by the wild Chigmit Mountains on the Cook Inlet side.

Mount Spurr, 11,100 feet, and Telaquana Mountain, 8,070 feet, stand as sentinels to two important breaks in this range which give access to the Bay region. Merrill Pass, 3,180 feet, has been important to air navigation since its discovery by pioneer flier R. H. Merrill in 1929, and 3,100-foot Telaquana Pass,

King Salmon Creek flows across lowlands on the Alaska Peninsula near Naknek. This view is in September, with mountains of the Aleutian Range in the distance. (James Faro)

*Clockwise from right*—Wind-whipped grass describes a circle in the Ukak River Delta, Katmai National Monument. / Fireweed (*Epilobium angustifolium*) grows near a downed cottonwood along the Brooks River, Katmai National Monument. / Wolverine Falls, 21 miles northeast of Mount Katmai in Katmai National Monument. (All photos by Nancy Simmerman)

Brown bear trail in a spruce forest at Katmai National Monument, on the Alaska Peninsula. On trails of moderate use, each bear will step in footprints made by the preceding bear . . . a habit that eventually wears deep ruts in the soft forest floor. See page 91 for additional information on Katmai National Monument. (Nancy Simmerman)

21

between the headwaters of the Neacola and Telaquana rivers, long has served as a foot trail for Interior Natives bound for Cook Inlet. Even more important to the Bristol Bay region is Lake Clark Pass, elevation 1,000 feet, which passes through the Aleutian Range from Cook Inlet to Lake Clark.

The Chigmit Mountains (6,000 to 8,000 feet) are lower than the neighboring Alaska Range, but present an imposing jumble of peaks, serrated ridges, spires, steep valleys and glacial fields. Access to Bristol Bay's lake country through the Chigmits is afforded by a portage road over 966-foot Summit Pass, from Iliamna Bay on the Cook Inlet side to Pile Bay on Iliamna Lake. The road is often used to transport gill-netters from Bristol Bay to Cook Inlet. There also is a longer, seldom-used foot trail that meanders 20 miles from Cottonwood Bay, near Iliamna Bay, to the shores of Iliamna Lake. (This route crosses summits of 1,700, 1,500 and 1,975 feet.)

Mountains along Bristol Bay's south and east boundaries rise between the moderate climate of Cook Inlet, with its abundant precipitation, fog and overcast skies, and the clearer, drier, colder weather of continental Alaska, where, temperature ranges can be extreme. A high of 84° and a low of -64° have been recorded at Iliamna; precipitation averages less than 20 inches along the lowlands on the western flank of the Chigmits, but rises to about 26 inches at Iliamna.

The Japan Current, which moderates the climate in the Aleutians, is missing in

*Opposite page—* Sockeye salmon enter Alexi Creek, part of the Newhalen River system, during a peak run in the fall of 1965. This photograph would be difficult to take again—runs have declined since 1965. *Below—*An unusual photograph taken over the shoreline of Ualik Lake. Each dark spot in the shallow water is a female sockeye building a gravel nest in which to spawn. Ualik Lake is the source of the Kanik River, 35 miles northwest of the village of Clarks Point. (Both photos by Ole Mathisen, U. W. Fisheries Research Institute)

Bristol Bay. Dillingham has recorded temperatures of from -41° to 92°, with an average of 26 inches of rain and 65 inches annual snowfall. Aleknagik has records of from -36° to 88°, with precipitation of 34 inches and 81 inches of snow, while Port Heiden shows extremes of from -25° to 82°, with 13 inches of rain and 29 inches of snow.

"Good weather is the exception and does not last long when it does occur," reports the U.S. Coast and Geodetic Survey's *Coast Pilot.* Bay winds are generally from the northeast from October to March and most frequently from the southwest during late spring, summer and early fall. The average wind velocity at Port Heiden is 15 knots. At Naknek near the head of Bristol Bay, the prevailing winds are northwest except in summer, with an average velocity of 10 knots. Inland the Lake Clark area averages 8- to 12-knot winds at lower elevations; north in winter and south in summer. Gusts of 100 miles an hour have been recorded in mountain passes, however, and severe storms buffet the area from December to March.

The growing season runs from 100 to 127 days and lack of permafrost in many areas makes gardening possible, if not profitable. Solid ice on the Bay can be expected between November and early April, and river freezeup and breakup usually precede the Bay by about two weeks. Iliamna Lake generally is frozen from late December until late May; Lake Clark melts by late May or early June. Smaller lakes tend to freeze a bit earlier and thaw sooner.

In total, the Bristol Bay region covers approximately 55,000 square miles, roughly the size of Ohio. More than half of the region is inland and, includes some of the most valuable and fascinating fresh-water lakes in Alaska. Iliamna and Becharof rank, respectively, the largest and second-largest lakes in the state. The Tikchik Lakes-Wood River area attracts hundreds of sports fishermen from all over the world. Lake Clark has been listed "among the most beautiful bodies of water in the world" by no lesser experts than

A September scene in the Wood River-Tikchik Lakes region, along the northern edge of the Bristol Bay region—a favorite area for outdoorspeople. (Nancy Simmerman)

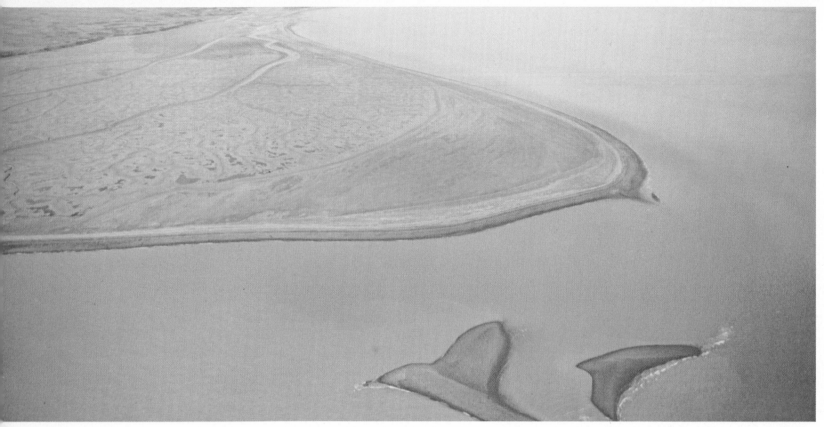

the usually reserved mapmakers of the U.S. Coast and Geodetic Survey. Ironically, Bristol Bay was about the last area in Alaska to receive the attention of surveyors. Iliamna Lake remained uncharted until 1961 and neighboring Lake Clark was partially fathomed in 1963. Another semi-blank is the area between Rainy Pass and Iliamna Lake. According to the National Park Service, which is trying to acquire the real estate, "the first geologic expedition into this area did little more than brush the western foothills and lakes regions of the Chigmit Mountains. Until the Geologic Survey expeditions of 1927-29, the mountains were almost totally unknown, geologically and otherwise. Little has changed since then."

There are similar vagaries concerning the Ahklun Mountains and even the coast—an area that has attracted fishermen from all over the world since the turn of the century. Consider this note on Chart 8802:

"The area between Cape Constantine

# Present charts are considerably in error . . . because the coast is in a constant state of flux.

*Opposite page*—Cape Constantine, on the southern tip of the Nushagak Peninsula, 48 miles southwest of Dillingham, juts boldly into Bristol Bay. The waters between Cape Constantine and Cape Newenham still have not been accurately surveyed, according to the *Coast Pilot*.

*Left*—Cape Newenham, at the northwestern corner of the Bristol Bay region, photographed after a snowfall in November. Cape Newenham, separating Kuskokwim and Bristol bays, was named in 1778 by a lieutenant who was sent ashore by English explorer Captain James Cook. According to Cook's log, the lieutenant "landed on the point, and, having climbed the highest hill, took possession of the country in his Majesty's name, and left on the hill a bottle, in which was described, on a piece of paper, the names of the ships and the date of discovery." (Bill Crocker)

*Below*—Hagemeister Island, in Togiak Bay between Cape Newenham and Cape Constantine (see previous page), is 24 miles long—largest island in the Bristol Bay region.
*Right*—A huge glacier seen on the flight through Lake Clark Pass, elevation 1,000 feet, the major air route from Cook Inlet through the Aleutian Range to the Lake Clark area. (Nancy Simmerman)

*Opposite page*—A major eruption belches ash from The Gas Rocks, on the shore of Becharof Lake, in April 1977. This form of eruption is known as a *maar*—a release of pressure through cracks in the earth—not a volcano. (Lou Gwartney)

and Cape Newenham is unsurveyed and there are indications that the present charts are considerably in error," confess authors of the *Coast Pilot*. But perhaps that's just as well, they continue, because the coast is in a state of constant flux.

"This is particularly true of the northeast arms and the approaches which receive the waters of the great salmon streams on which the Bering Sea canneries are located. The rivers discharge a great quantity of water into wide indentations which open on the arms of the great bay. The discolored water of some rivers is charged with a large amount of sediment which when deposited forms shoal areas." ("Shoal areas" is a nice name for mud—and you have never

*seen* mud until you've had it suck your boots off at the mouth of the Nushagak, the Naknek, or just about any other river along the shores of Bristol Bay.)

The land, too, is subject to change, for the country is young yet. Within the recent past, for example, a glacier that historically has blocked Lake Clark Pass suddenly receded. At Becharof Lake an incredible eruption appeared at The Gas Rocks, a spectacular rock bluff on the south shore, blackening the sky with ash for more than a week.

And, like the region itself, land ownership is constantly changing. There are an estimated 4 to 4.6 million acres (15% to 18%) physically suited for settlement, which gives Bristol Bay area more potential for use and development than any subregion in the state. However, only 8,560 acres are in private hands, about 26 million have recently been selected by Native corporations and the rest is being quibbled over by state and federal agencies. Ownership patterns, especially around the big lakes, are so checkerboarded as to make future management unwieldy, if not impossible.

# Earlier Times on the Bay

It would appear that even in aboriginal times, Bristol Bay was one of the last open frontiers, attracting restless adventurers, malcontents and those seeking a loss of identity from many other areas . . . people who came, but rarely settled for long.

The Aglegmiut, Yupik Eskimos whom explorers found living at the mouth of the Nushagak River and down the coast to Port Heiden, had in better days been known as the "Warrior People," holding Nelson Island and ruthlessly seeking to expand their territory. Instead, according to pioneer Indian missionary John Kilbuck on the Kuskokwim, they suffered a stunning defeat and remnants of the tribe sought refuge in the Bay region, ultimately turning to Russian traders for protection.

The Aglegmiut were pursued by waves of vengeful Togiamiut Yupiks who lived in the Togiak Bay and Togiak River area. At the same time, aggressive Aleuts from islands to the southwest sought to invade their southern boundaries.

Upriver the Nushagagmiut Eskimos settled in the less coveted interior Tikchik Lakes-Wood River area, venturing to the Bay in fishing season, and the Kiatagmiut of the Kvichak River and Iliamna Lake region likewise descended on the Aglegmiut . . . sometimes to war and sometimes to trade.

Inland, the Tanaina Athabascans of the great northern lakes, rugged glacier country and barren Lime Hills expanded in number and courage to take on all comers, becoming the only interior Indians to reach the sea. Today they speculate that, spared the coming of the white man, they might well have conquered all.

The first whites to see the country and return to report were with Captain James Cook aboard the *Resolution*, July 9, 1778. Cook was disappointed when his hoped-for Northwest Passage was blocked by a barrier of flat, low-lying Bay shore. Shoal water discouraged landing

*Opposite page*—The framework of a replica sod house (*barabara*) on display at Katmai National Monument. (Nancy Simmerman) *Inset photo*, taken about 1890 along the Naknek River, shows Eskimo women in front of a *barabara*. (Smithsonian Institution) *Above*—An unidentified man poses for a photographer (also unidentified) in the Bristol Bay region. The photo was taken before 1887, perhaps by Hartmann and Weinland. (Smithsonian Institution)

# Captain Cook: It (Bristol Bay) must abound with salmon, as we saw many leaping in the sea before the entrance. . . .

but Cook named the place Bristol (River) after home ground and carefully logged a hint of its future:

"It [Bristol Bay] must abound with salmon, as we saw many leaping in the sea before the entrance and some were found in the maws of cod which we caught."

Russian landowners may have entered the territory from the back door via Cook Inlet in 1791 when Demitri Ivanovich Bocharov explored the northern Alaska Peninsula. Russians were said to have established a trading station in the Iliamna area about the turn of the century but legend has it that bands of Athabascans, united when traders mistreated them, wiped out the post and killed all except one boy, the son of a Russian leader. (These same Indians later braved glaciers and Cook Inlet tides to trade at distant Kenai after that post was built in 1793.)

Nushagak Bay Eskimos in the 1890's.
(Smithsonian Institution)

32

Some of the old ways survive. These fish-skin boots were made by a Native woman in Nondalton, 15 miles north of Iliamna.

At about the same time Father Juvenal was dispatched by the Russian Orthodox bishop of Irkutsk to Ilyamna Station over objections of Kenai Indians, who argued they needed him more and that the Ilyamnas were "very bad." And so it would seem—the interior Indians murdered the priest, reportedly because he dallied with one of their women.

According to historian Hubert Bancroft (1886), "It had been a marvel to the savages that a man [Juvenal] should put a bridle upon his passions and live in celibacy, but their wonder was mingled with feelings of respect. To overcome the influence which the missionary was gaining over his people, Shakmut [the local chief] plotted to throw temptation in

his way, and alas for Juvenal . . . it must be related that he fell. In the dead of night, according to his own confession, an Ilyamna damsel captured him by storm."

Juvenal's diary supposedly was preserved by his assistant, a boy named Kinita, who presented it with the priest's papers to Father Veniaminof who visited Nushagak 33 years after the fact. Some historians claim the diary is a fake but Indian legend backs it, pinpointing the site of the murder as Priest Rock, near Kijik on Lake Clark.

Russian maps of this period are fuzzy about the Bay area and, as one of his last acts as governor, Alexander Baranof dispatched an expedition (1818), directing Petr Krosakovskiy to open new areas for fur trade and also to keep an eye out for a lost colony of Russians—descendants of the Deshnev party, which set across Bering Strait in the direction of Seward Peninsula in 1648. No descendants were found but a fort and trading post were built at Nushagak, and the settlers were soon doing a brisk business in swans' down, sea otter pelts, caribou skins and walrus ivory.

Another trading post was established in

A Russian Orthodox cross in a graveyard at Naknek. (Nancy Simmerman)

the area but met with no success and Nushagak Redoubt later dwindled in importance due to extreme silting of its harbor and establishment of more easily accessible ports on the Kuskokwim.

In 1821 A. K. Etolin, a Finn in the service of the Russians, was dispatched in the *Baranof*, with Vasiliy Khromchenko in the *Golovnin*, to map the coast. Both commanders, put off by the shallow waters of the Bay, did little shore reconnaissance but managed to chart waters in the neighborhood of Hagemeister Island and garner secondhand reports of life on the Bay from neighboring Eskimos of the Kuskokwim:

"The Aglegmiut lead exactly the same kind of ife as do all the peoples inhabiting Kenai Gulf, Kodiak Island and the lands to the North of them," Khromchenko reported in his journal. "It is difficult to determine the temper of the oppressed Aglegmiut. They now seem quite peaceful, but this may be involuntary. Other people tell many stories of their obstinacy and barbarity." He added that these Eskimos believed in shamans, lived by the sea with occasional forays to hunt caribou, traded

beluga whale, sealskin and blubber for beaver and otter with inland Indians, traveled by dog team and lived in mud huts like the Aleuts.

In 1829 explorer Ivan Filippovich Vasiliev traveled to the North Nushagak region with three Russians, six company Aleuts and ten Aglegmiuts who were loyal by virtue of the fact that their families were being held hostage at the fort. However, the Natives refused to go beyond Tikchik—fearful of the terrible Kuskokwagmiut—and Vasiliev had to regroup; he finally made it to the Kuskokwim the following year.

Russian priests sometimes traveled the river network but their records are fragmentary: The first full-fledged Russian Orthodox church wasn't established in the interior until 1881 (at Kijik) and earlier, at the time of the sale of Alaska to the United States in 1867, it is clear that the Russians still knew little about the Bay.

**I**n his *State of Alaska* (1954), the late Senator Ernest Gruening observed that "salmon and Alaska have been as closely intertwined as cotton and the South" and Bristol Bay lies in the very heartland—Atlanta—the world's richest sockeye spawning area.

The Bay languished for some time under U.S. protection. The year of the purchase, Captain J. W. White, commander of the U.S. Revenue cutter *Wayanda*, reported that the old Russian trading post at Nushagak had been purchased by the Alaska Commercial Company and a mail run had been established overland from Saint Michael to Nushagak—then by water to Sitka. Beyond this little was heard from the western front until the founding of the salmon industry.

Russians had been slow to realize the food potential of the Bay and had only begun to gear up for commercial fishing when the territory was sold. John W. Clark, chief of the Nushagak trading post under early American ownership, may have operated a saltery at Clarks Point,

but the first major enterprise was that of the schooner *Neptune*, which prospected Nushagak Bay in 1883 and salted a large number of fish. Arctic Pack Company built a cannery at Nushagak that same year and in 1884 produced 400 cases of salmon.

In 1885 Alaska Packing Company of Astoria established the "Scandinavian" cannery on the west side of Nushagak Bay, with a capacity of 2,000 cases per day; it operated until the end of the Second World War. Bristol Bay Canning Company, called Bradford Cannery, went into production a few miles from the Scandinavian in 1886 at a site which later became Dillingham. Nushagak Packing Company built at Clarks Point two years later, closed from 1892 to 1900, then reopened with a larger facility.

By 1897 the fishing industry had invested $867,000 in the Bay and in 1908 there were ten canneries in operation at Nushagak with more at Naknek; on the Igushik, Kvichak and Ugashik rivers; at Egegik, Ekuk, Herendeen Bay, Togiak and Nelson Lagoon.

That same year, to add to the excitement, there was a gold stampede to the Mulchatna River. It turned out to be

Influence of the Russian Orthodox Church has been considerable in the region. Shown here is the interior of the church at Igiugig, on the Kvichak River 46 miles southwest of Iliamna.

*Frank Leslie's Illustrated Newspaper* dispatched an expedition in 1890-91 to probe the Bristol Basy region, with Alfred B. Schanz, astronomer-writer-historian, in the company of local resident John Clark and others. Predictably, the expedition received front-page treatment in the weekly paper.

TWENTY PAGES.

# FRANK LESLIE'S ILLUSTRATED NEWSPAPER

No. 1829.—Vol. LXXI]    NEW YORK—FOR THE WEEK ENDING DECEMBER 13, 1890.    [PRICE, 10 CENTS.

THE "FRANK LESLIE'S ILLUSTRATED NEWSPAPER" EXPLORATION OF ALASKA—DESCENDING THE ALASCK RIVER.
FROM A DRAWING BY K. J. GLAVE.—(See Page 362.)

little more than a flash in the pan, but it generated government interest in the interior, which still was little known.

In 1881 the U.S. Army Signal Corps established a station at Nushagak. Manager Charles McKay traveled widely, but when he drowned mysteriously two years later, he left no record of his exploration.

Between 1887 and 1888 a party of Yukon prospectors wandered down the Mulchatna to the Nushagak, but again no written record was preserved. The U.S. Fish Commission steamer *Albatross* finally surveyed the coast in 1890 and a Bristol Bay chapter was added to the *Coast Pilot* in 1891, but the interior remained a blank on the map. Enter the *Frank Leslie's Illustrated Newspaper* Expedition (1890-91) with astronomer-writer-historian Alfred B. Schanz in the company of local trader John Clark.

"I had heard vague stories about the existence of a large lake north of Iliamna," Schanz wrote, "and it seemed to Mr. Clark and myself best to follow up the tributaries of the Nushagak until we had traced one of its sources to the very watershed separating the Nushagak drainage basin from that of the great Lake Iliamna."

It proved the wrong way to go and the party, traveling in the dead of winter, grew "rather worse for wear" with "icicles six inches long congealed on [their] eyelashes." They ran out of food, sled dogs starved and the Eskimo guide admitted he didn't have a clue as to where they were. When at last Lake Clark was found they suffered the final shock of discovering their chosen "wilderness" was rather civilized. The Indian who ultimately led them to safety was wearing blue jeans, and the local village chief lived in a clean, modern house and served tea in a store-bought pot.

Mapping and mineral exploration followed. Josiah Spurr covered the upper Nushagak to Kulukak Bay for the U.S. Geological Survey in 1898. Wilfred Osgood toured Iliamna, Chulitna and Nushagak in 1902 for the Department of Agriculture. The U.S. Bureau of Fisheries began to explore salmon-spawning areas in earnest in 1907 and the U.S. Geological Survey sent parties to the lakes in 1909, and 1911; and to the Chulitna, Mulchatna, Holitna rivers and the Lime Hills in 1914.

Despite these surveys and a modest influx of trappers and prospectors, the area never really opened up. Early in 1901 the Trans-Alaska Company surveyed a winter sled route from Iliamna down the Mulchatna and Nushagak but decided traffic did not warrant installation of roadhouses. That same year surveys began for a railroad from Anvik on the Yukon to Lake Clark. The route, which included the Chulitna, was actually filed with the general land office in 1912 and given consideration by the Alaska Railroad Commission, but the only construction was a few pilings at Lake Clark.

Steamer service to Iliamna Bay (on Cook Inlet) and Koggiung on Bristol Bay began at the time of the Mulchatna gold rush but was short-lived. In fact, scheduled transport to the outside world could not be counted on from the Bay area until the mid-1930's, when weekly plane service to Anchorage was initiated.

One reason was that the salmon industry fell on hard times, largely due to heavy fishing and poor market conditions. Despite repeated warnings from local delegates, Congress turned a deaf ear on

# Preachers far outnumber artists, but not necessarily because heaven is more inspiring than the local scenery

Betsy Nowatak of Kokhanok shows off a beautiful parka and her pup, Princess. The village—population 28 in the last census—is on the south shore of Iliamna Lake.

40

# People and Communities

The last census reported 4,632 people living in the Bristol Bay region in 24 villages, the city of Dillingham and military installation at King Salmon. (Bristol Bay Native Corporation also includes the communities of Chignik, Chignik Lagoon, Chignik Lake, Ivanof Bay and Perryville, but because they are on the south side of the Alaska Peninsula and outside of the true geographical region, they are not included in this report.) About one-third of the population is white; two-thirds are of Eskimo, Aleut or Athabascan extraction.

Although the population count showed a 16.7% increase over the previous decade, the natural increase in the wider census division indicates there has been an outmigration of 18.5% for nonwhites. This is understandable since median family income for Bristol Bay recently was

*Above*—Egegik is on the north shore of the Alaska Peninsula, near the mouth of the Egegik River. Population is about 150. (Neil and Betty Johannsen)
*Left*—Pete Koktelash of Nondalton wears a handsome beaver-skin vest.

41

*Clockwise from right*—Fred Hurley of Ekwok, on the Nushagak River, shows off a giant turnip from his garden. / Fast-growing Naknek, on the north coast of the Alaska Peninsula, 56 miles southeast of Dillingham. On the opposite bank of the Naknek River is South Naknek. Naknek's population has increased considerably since the last census figure of 250. / Oldest resident of the region was Evon Olympic of South Naknek, said to have been born about 1860, shown here celebrating his 119th birthday. Olympic died in 1977. (J. Scott Carter) / Pedro Bay on Iliamna Lake 21 miles east of the village of Iliamna, had a population of 53 in the last census.

reported to be $7,800 as compared with $12,400 for the state, and that the median income for Native families was under $6,000.

The major source of money here is fishing and during the census year (1970) only 450 jobs were reported in that field, with 700 in fish processing. Just previous to and following this period, the salmon industry suffered disastrous setbacks due to poor runs. By 1978 the catch was up and so were the prices. Native corporations have invested heavily in the area, private interest is high and government projects are also on the increase, creating a building boom and many new jobs in the major service centers of Naknek and Dillingham. However, some residents still manage to live primarily off the land.

It's best, when visiting Bristol Bay, not to ask anyone what he does for work. The answer is often "seasonal." Steady salaries, like three consecutive days of good weather, cannot be relied on and the typical Bay resident is, by necessity, a jack-of-all-trades. Even the best-known, local-boy-made-good, Governor Jay Hammond, has a job resume that reads like an employment agency sampler: sometime guide, sometime pilot, sometime fish and game agent and occasional politician.

Or consider Gillie Jacko, who in his own sphere is certainly as famous as the governor. Jacko is a bear killer of legendary proportion. Now in his 70's and having a bit of trouble with his eyes, it's become Jacko's custom to let a bear approach within a short distance for a really good look, then plug the bruin with characteristic accuracy.

Born in Indian country north at Whitefish Lake of an Eskimo mother and Athabascan father, Jacko recalls traveling at the age of nine with his father and grandfather via skin boat all the way down the Kuskokwim to Crooked Creek and Bethel to visit his mother's people.

"I never went to school but I did pretty good," he reflects. He's taken whatever paying jobs came along, fished and seen more real wilderness at closer range than just about any person around. He settled finally at Pedro Bay.

Problems? A few, he admits. Like last spring when a big brown messed up his trapping cabin across the lake.

The Gillie Jackos in front of their place at Pedro Bay, on Iliamna Lake.

43

*Clockwise from lower left*—Port Heiden, population about 75, on the north shore of the Alaska Peninsula. / Grant Vanoy and his cabin at Pope-Vanoys Landing. / A portion of King Salmon, viewed from the airport tower. Population of the town, 15 miles southeast of Naknek, is about 300. / Iliamna, on Iliamna Lake, had a population of about 50 in the last census.

"Broke in through the window and took out 50 pounds of sugar. I had honey in little plastic bottles and he bit holes in them to suck the honey out. Boy, he just made me mad!"

But the charm of the country is worth such minor inconveniences, he reflects. "And there's nothing to be scared of in the world so long as I have my .30-.30."

The Pope-Vanoy family, of Pope-Vanoys Landing near Copper River, also admire the bounty of Iliamna, not just for hunting but for farming. Art Pope and his wife gave up a chance at a lucrative pension in Ohio to move there in 1954 after their son discovered the land. They were followed by Mrs. Pope's brother, Grant Vanoy, and eventually enough grandchildren, nieces and nephews to make the place an official mail drop. The families live pretty much off their farming miracles, producing everything for their table from soup to noodles, to herbs, teas and spices.

Others also do well at interior farming.

Nels Hedlund of Chekok and a small sled built for his grandchild. Hedlund has probably mushed more miles than any other human being, having spent years carrying the mail through the lower Kuskokwim Region.

Floyd Dennison came to Lake Clark with his father, Charlie, to prospect for gold back in 1932 and stayed on to create fine gardens with salmon-gut fertilizer and sawdust from their lumbermill.

The Hornbergers, who have prime land across the lake, have worked hard to develop a good wind-generation system for their electricity, and have helped inspire others with their healthy garden. The Hurley family of Ekwok has farmed the same fields on the Nushagak since the

Twin Hills, a small village next to low hills of the same name.

Top—The waterfront at the village of New Stuyahok, on the Nushagak River, 52 miles northeast of Dillingham. Population is about 150. (Neil and Betty Johannsen) Above—Koliganek, on the Nushagak River, 65 miles northeast of Dillingham, has about 100 residents. (Neil and Betty Johannsen)

turn of the century. Nels and Rose Hedlund, an Athabascan-Eskimo match, furnish eggs to the Iliamna area as well as sled dogs and freight sleds to enthusiastic mushers throughout Alaska. This is one area where dog teams never were totally replaced by snow machines and Nels, who used to run mail by dog team over the Kuskokwim, still favors that mode of transportation.

"One thing about dogs," he reasons, "they never break down and they never run out of gas."

Professionals, too, are into this life style. B. J. Hill and her husband Pete, who teach at Kokhanok, refuse to plumb or wire the handsome new house they just built on Iliamna Lake and for all their higher education are raising their four children much as Pete was raised by his Athabascan mother. B. J. is president of the local mushers' association. Pete flies his own plane, and hunting is one of the prerequisites of living in a village with no store. In addition, the whole clan packs up and goes commercial fishing in Bristol Bay each summer, as do many inlanders.

"It's been awfully easy country to get along in until just recently," reminisces Paul Romie, sometime trapper, fisherman and postmaster at Ekwok. "Where else could you work just one month and live for a whole year?"

Indeed, it is the wealth of the Bay, the lure of that lucrative salmon season, that unites the interior with the coast, bringing families hundreds of miles downriver to become neighbors for the summer with coast dwellers.

Tom Chythlook of Aleknagik tries out a traditional skin boat on Lake Aleknagik. The kayak is just for fun—he usually travels in a skiff with a 50-horsepower engine.

Who fishes? Just about everybody. The area is rich in Scandinavians, Italians and Orientals whose families came with the early salmon industry two or three generations ago. The mayor of Dillingham, Freeman Roberts, heads to sea whenever he gets a chance. The governor's wife tends a set net. Tom Chythlook, who still uses his skin-covered kayak to hunt ducks at Aleknagik Lake, travels to the Bay with a 50-horse engine and skiff. College kids, housewives and grandmothers rush to the action. Career government employees at King Salmon parlay vacation time into the vocation. Military men from all over the world plan maneuvers at King Salmon Air Force Station for this season—so much so that the base commander quips he'd like to rename the place "Mud Flats." And Elmer "Red" Harrop, who gave it all up to take the post as magistrate in Naknek, feels vaguely restless not to be governed by the tides.

*Above*—Nondalton, on the west shore of Sixmile Lake, is 15 miles north of Iliamna. Population of the village was 205 in the last census.
*Left*—Levelock, 58 miles east of Dillingham, is on the bank of the Kvichak River. Population was 88 in 1970.

Port Alsworth, on Lake Clark, long-time home of Babe and Mary Alsworth (and others). Babe, a legendary bush pilot in the region, shocked everyone by retiring to Hawaii not long ago.

Big fishing money has been hard to come by in recent years, especially for many inlanders who discovered they were not eligible for recently instituted limited entry permits because fishing was so poor in the years set to qualify that it did not pay a family from the interior to travel so far. Also, overhead has risen so that it's possible to invest thousands of dollars in gear, only to go bust when the season closes almost before it starts for want of salmon.

Things were so tight in 1974 that President Nixon declared Bristol Bay a disaster area and a Regional Development Council was formed to seek options to the fishing industry. Few have been found to date and, anyway, it's more than the lure of big money that makes fishing important to Bay people.

"I've worked in the oil fields and it's not much fun," considers Dillingham Mayor Freeman Roberts. "You've got people born in the villages and all they want to do is go fishing. They're happy at it. They don't want to go into construction work. They don't want to leave home. Fishermen want to fish!"

Nor are Bay salmon the only quarry.

Sport fishing lodges, dedicated to the rainbow, grayling, char, lake trout and other species, dot the lakes and are run by some of the state's most zealous fishermen. Bob Curtis, owner of Tikchik Narrows Lodge, is so fanatical about fish, friends sometimes ask him how he can bear to kill them.

"I don't kill many. Let them go," he admits. And when the season is over and he's guided his umpteenth hundredth sport fisherman, what does he do for vacation?

"Why, I go fishing," he replies, startled that there might be other alternatives.

In the early days, trapping was a viable option and some still pursue it, though more for recreational and sentimental reasons than for profit. One of the original hangers-on is Ole Wassenkari, 79, who settled on the Kvichak in the 1920's, when "pretty near every creek had a trapping cabin and there were some on the lake in every bay. But all the young guys took off

Clockwise from left—Dillingham is the largest settlement in the region, and probably the fastest growing. (Population in 1970 was 424; estimated population in early 1978 was 1,269.) The town is at the junction of the Wood and Nushagak rivers, and long has been the principal supply point for other Nushagak Bay communities. (John Laner) / Aleknagik, on the southeast shore of Lake Aleknagik, is 17 miles north of Dillingham. Population was about 225 in the last census. / A dog team races through Dillingham during the Beaver Roundup, largest wintertime festival in the Bristol Bay region. (James Faro) / Ole Wassenkari, who lives on the Kvichak River at Ole Creek, shows off some new potatoes in his garden. Wassenkari, 79, still runs a modest trapline, supplementing his income with four gardens.

49

during World War II and they didn't come back."

Long known as the strongest man in Bristol Bay, Wassenkari still runs a modest trapline and supplements his income by farming four sizable gardens without power tools. Friends have been urging him to join them at the Pioneers' Home, but he has a strong affinity for his isolated river country and argues that "there's still too much work to do at Ole Creek" to consider a vacation.

Surprisingly, flying is also considered a traditional Bay occupation, because bush pilots became important to this roadless country early—about the time Wassenkari settled on the Kvichak, in fact.

One of the most colorful pilots is homesteader-farmer Babe Alsworth, whose old aircraft has almost been as familiar a sight in lake country as the eagles. In 1977, to the astonishment of neighbors, Babe and Mary left their bush airline in the hands of son Glen, and retired to garden in Hawaii. It was the doings of writer Richard Proenneke of *One Man's Wilderness* fame (please see ad on page 96), who gave Babe a set of vacation tickets in return for faithful charter service to Proenneke's remote wilderness cabin at Twin Lakes. A number of locals express betrayal at this loss of local color but there are other living legends to carry on: Gruff, cigar-chomping George Tibbits Sr. out of Naknek, who mercifully barks worse than he bites—quiet, unassuming Alex Griechen, a Pilot Point Native and his son-in-law, the feisty Monty Hand—super-cool Orin Seybert of Ugashik, who pioneered routes from the

Bay to the Aleutians—Don Johnson, who alternates landings on the beach at Port Moller and a homemade strip at Bear Lake with stag hunting in Argentina—and Trygve Olson, a local boy, who initiated air service at Iliamna in 1967 with one plane and has expanded his fleet to six.

Also, there is Dick Armstrong of Dillingham, whose son represents the third generation of Armstrongs in the air-taxi business, and Roy Smith, who won his first plane in a poker game, taught himself to fly and logged thousands of hours in the region. (When Smith's son and daughter-in-law were killed in a crash, he sold out to lifelong Alaska Peninsula residents Martin Severson and Artie and Marlene Johnson.)

Perhaps it's all that flying but the Bristol Bay area is more heavily into religion than most. Seventh-Day Adventists homesteaded at Aleknagik in the 1930's. Port Alsworth on Lake Clark has been influenced by the Arctic Bible Mission, which also claims considerable territory on Iliamna. And Russian Orthodoxy, with some Moravian competition, has a foothold on the Bay and along the river systems.

*Clockwise from left*—Bush pilot Don Johnson with his air taxi at Bear Lake, where he has a homemade strip. / Old Nushagak, at Nushagak Point 6 miles south of Dillingham. / Richard Proenneke in his cabin with a friendly camp robber. Proenneke's life at Twin Lakes was chronicled in *One Man's Wilderness*, by Sam Keith.

51

*Clockwise from above*—Port Moller is at the southwesternmost corner of the Bristol Bay basin, on the north shore of the Alaska Peninsula. The village, with a population of 33 in the last census, was established as a cannery in 1916. / Hundreds of glass floats in skiffs at Nelson Lagoon, on a lagoon of the same name, 20 miles west of the village of Port Moller. (Robert Gill Jr.) / Togiak, with a population of 220 in the last census, is at the head of Togiak Bay, two miles west of the mouth of the Togiak River. The village is the largest west of Dillingham in the Bristol Bay region. (Neil and Betty Johannsen) / Linda Behnke, of Port Alsworth, displays a mosquitoproof backpack she made for her new baby.

Preachers far outnumber the artists—and not necessarily because heaven is more inspiring than the local scenery. Ted Lambert, well-established Alaskan painter, elected to spend his final years on the Kvichak but produced little during this period, preferring to live off the land as most people do.

Current exceptions are the carvers of Togiak who do traditional Eskimo work in ivory and an imaginative Eskimo immigrant from Goodnews Bay, Sam Fox, who combines the no-nonsense craftsmanship of his ancestors with superb humor and a style that is decidedly modern.

Another new talent is Michael Christensen, formerly of California, who came to the Bay to fish and took up painting, while recovering from a broken leg, to present the beauty of the area with rare whimsy in masterful watercolor.

And did you catch the phrase "formerly of" and the word "immigrant"? You hear more and more about newcomers around the Bay these days for, despite the hardship statistics, increasing numbers of people—especially from crowded urban areas—are learning of the charm of the place.

Tim and Marilyn Crace, for example, moved from Anchorage to Pedro Bay to give their children wilderness experience. Judy and John Travlos went to Port Moller for good wages at the RCA site and have decided to stay even though the site and their job have been declared obsolete. Easygoing, unflappable Vi Hasti and her family came to Dillingham from Kenai during a construction boom and decided to make it home. Vi manages the local hotel, her husband works construction and like most "city" folks on the Bay, they tend set nets in season.

It is Mrs. Hasti, perhaps, who best sums up the spirit. Her family came for the money . . . decided to stay because of the fine school system . . . and for something less tangible.

"I never met a stranger here," she marvels. And that is surely the mark of the Bay.

Eskimo dolls made by Sam Fox, Dillingham artist—one of several craftspeople producing innovative work on the bay.

The old-timers here say that the small birds ride south on the backs of their larger brothers. . . . No one has seen this celestial hitchhiking, but legend has it, and the old-timers swear it is true

An Arctic tern feeds its young at Nelson Lagoon, at the extreme southwestern corner of the Bristol Bay region. (Robert Gill Jr.)

# Rich Wilderness

Spring is noisy and spectacular in Bristol Bay—especially the arrival of a quarter of a million migrating birds, hurrying to the business of making nests and raising young in the lush but brief Alaska summer. They come with the first open water from wintering areas as far away as Russia, Japan, Mexico, South America, New Zealand and the South Pacific Islands; and the roll call is exotic. . . .

Welcome the glaucous, mew and Sabine's gulls, Arctic terns, long-tailed and parasitic jaegers, bar-tailed godwits, pelagic and red-faced cormorants, marbled murrelets and pigeon guillemots.

Some, like the emperor and Canada geese, and brightly colored eiders, linger only until breakup, then head for the High Arctic. Others, including golden and black-bellied plovers, western

Whistling swans displaying in the Naknek River; photo was taken in May. (Richard Russell)

55

sandpipers, dunlins, turnstones and phalaropes, camp on the hummocks and along beaches for the season. Many tundra ponds boast a resident swan family; sandhill cranes congregate by the riversides and almost every lake has loons. Aerial surveys made in the Bristol Bay region, including the Nushagak, show a breeding population of 32 ducks and 1.2 swans per square mile in the

lowland—141 species counted in all, including the mallard, American widgeon, harlequin, green-winged teal, shoveler, gadwall, American goldeneye, bufflehead, red-breasted merganser and Steller's eider.

Inland there's a comic little fellow the old-timers call the ouzel (known also as the dipper), who can be seen casually strolling underwater along clear stream bottoms in search of lunch. Here, too, among the 103 species counted at Iliamna Lake alone, nest the peregrine falcon, bald eagle, gyrfalcon and osprey. Not to mention the magpie, redpoll, Canada jay, pine grosbeak, white-winged crossbill, three-toed woodpecker, chickadee, several varieties of owls, and more.

Only a few—the white-tailed, rock and willow ptarmigans, the spruce grouse, the raven and hardier sea birds—stay during the winter. For most, this is just a way stop along the Arctic Bird Migration Route, the Mid-Pacific Route and the Great North American Pacific Flyway. And in the fall, when the ranks of feathered tourists are swelled by fledglings of summer, their exodus is truly spectacular. Great swans and

dun-colored sandhill cranes crowd overhead, the joyful honk of southbound geese reaches raucous proportions and suddenly all the small birds fly up to join the migrants, vanishing as quickly as they came.

The old-timers here say that the small birds—by nature's prearrangement—ride south on the backs of their larger brothers . . . or perhaps in their windstream. No one has seen this celestial hitchhiking, but legend has it, and the old-timers swear it is true.

*Clockwise from left*—A black-legged kittiwake and its rather large youngster on a nest at Herendeen Bay, 12 miles southwest of Port Moller. (Robert Gill Jr.) / Parakeet auklets, photographed in early July on a remote island in Bristol Bay. (Rollie Ostermick) / Common murres crowd the top of a rocky perch in Bristol Bay. (Rollie Ostermick) / Emperor geese at Nelson Lagoon, on the lower north side of the Alaska Peninsula. (Robert Gill Jr.)

A bull moose, with snow on its antlers, photographed in October along the Alaska Peninsula. Moose have been hunted heavily, and their numbers have dropped sharply over the past decade. *Opposite page*—A lynx on the Alaska Peninsula, photographed in October. The animal had been preening itself dry, and sat for about 10 minutes while the photographer took pictures. (Both photos by Rollie Ostermick)

58

**I**n recently compiled proposals, which suggest setting aside vast areas of Bristol Bay for wildlife refuges, sanctuaries and parks, there are surprising voids regarding game populations—no accurate counts on moose, grizzly or black bears, Dall sheep, or for the unusual colonies of fresh-water seals in the lakes.

Residents will tell you most game species are on the decline due to heavy pressure from Outside trophy seekers—often from Anchorage—and because of pressures from increasing numbers of local residents. Natives of Nondalton, who used to count on bagging their moose on a nearby riverbank, now complain they must travel a hundred miles or so to fill their larders. The State Board of Game recently severely limited the taking of beaver, although it's believed a hardy population still exists in the more remote river drainages to the north. Walrus hunting has been curtailed, although the walrus population is thought to be nearly at an all-time high. And the Mulchatna caribou herd has long been considered one of the smaller in the state.

Despite this concern—or perhaps because of it—Bristol Bay is one of the most exciting areas in Alaska for observing wildlife. During an afternoon on a Port Moller beach, the casual stroller can usually spot a couple of scavenging brown bears (with tracks wider than the length of his foot); a few gray whales swimming close in to scratch the barnacles off their bellies; seals, beluga whales, fox, ground squirrels and a few curious strays from the caribou herd.

The region hosts 32 species of land mammals, ranging from the shrew, the world's smallest, to the Alaska brown bear, largest land carnivore of them all.

Concentrations of moose are found from the wooded southwestern shores of Iliamna Lake to the foothills of rugged mountain country and clear through the caribou lands in the south. Chulitna Flats, west of Lake Clark, are thought to be a prime moose calving area and—along with the Upper Talarik Creek drainage of Iliamna Lake and the Kijik River—is a heavily used wintering ground.

The Mulchatna caribou herd, one of

two in the region, is estimated at 3,000 to 5,000 animals. Calving area for the herd is between Telaquana Lake and Twin Lakes, where the hills are so ribbed with trails that they look like corduroy from the air. The second group, the Peninsula herd, is reportedly made up of smaller animals, perhaps because of interbreeding with reindeer. (The number of animals in both herds is down considerably from the not-distant past.)

Brown bears range from coastal beaches to the alpine zone, while black bears are found from Iliamna area and north. Early explorers reported large concentrations of bears in the Togiak area but these animals have been hunted heavily.

Bears emerge from their dens, usually at timber line on northerly slopes, in April and May to forage in grass and sedge flats. Spawning salmon attract them to stream areas in the fall and they return to their dens to sleep off the feast in November and December.

Dall sheep are found throughout the northern mountain area and have been reported as far south as Pedro Mountain, overlooking Pedro Bay. Little is known about their winter habits but as many as 600 animals have been spotted in this season north of the outlet for lower Twin Lake.

Fur bearers—beaver, mink, muskrat, marten, fox, river otter, lynx, wolverine, muskrat, weasel and ground squirrel— are found in upriver areas, although not as plentifully as in the past. Hares and porcupines also are present in reassuring numbers.

Iliamna is one of the few lakes in North America to host fresh-water harbor seals.

*Opposite page*—A caribou herd near Becharof Lake, southeast of Egegik on the Alaska Peninsula. In May 1977, 6,000 caribou were counted in the Mulchatna herd. More recent surveys show only 3,000 to 5,000 animals. (James Faro) *Center*—A red fox nurses its kit, about three weeks old, on the Alaska Peninsula. (Rollie Ostermick) *Left*—Its fur encrusted with snow and ice, a brown bear runs across a field during a snowstorm. The photograph was taken in October on the Alaska Peninsula. (Rollie Ostermick)

Islands along the north side of Bristol Bay—especially those guarding Togiak Bay—are heavily populated by marine mammals and birds. Most conspicuous is the male walrus, who seasonally migrates south to Bristol Bay . . . but no farther. (Where do the females go? No one seems to know for sure, but they are not often seen in Bristol Bay.)

*Right*—The walrus population is now high in Bristol Bay, apparently fully recovered from the heavy hunting for ivory that began in the 1800's. (Rollie Ostermick)

*Opposite page, top*—A male walrus on Round Island. (James Faro)

*Bottom*—Close-up of a bewhiskered bull walrus. (Rollie Ostermick)

The colony, which remains year-round, has peaked at about 150 but may now be smaller because of hunting pressure and recent hard winters.

With the coming of white traders in the late 1800's, the Bristol Bay walrus population was hunted to near extinction for its ivory, but a recent comeback has the population near an all-time high. For no reason scientists can fathom, the resident walruses that haul out on the Walrus Islands off Togiak are exclusively male; little is known about the females.

To the distress of local fishermen, the salt-water seal population is outstandingly healthy (due in part to passage of the Marine Mammal Protection Act of 1972), and beluga whales also appear in boggling numbers to pursue salmon runs. Biologists have tried using recordings of sounds made by killer whales—mortal enemy of the beluga—to frighten the white whales away from river mouths during the crucial spawning season.

The Kvichak
River system provides the single most
important spawning and rearing habitat
for red salmon in the world, according to
the National Park Service, which is
hoping to include this nursery in its
protective custody.

"From 1960 to 1969 this drainage
contributed 55% of the red salmon caught
in Bristol Bay, 33% of the entire U.S.
catch and 16% of the total world catch,"
according to a federal estimate.

The salmon season begins in early June
with the king run, which peaks in late
June about the time the red salmon run
starts. Chum salmon arrive about the
same time as the reds, and silvers appear
in mid-July and run through August. Pink
runs are best in even years from mid-June
through mid-August.

Kings are fewer in number than other
species but prized for their size (average

This brown bear, wading through an Alaska Peninsula stream
filled with spawning sockeye salmon, has trouble deciding
which fish to feed on. (Rollie Ostermick)

weight is 15-20 pounds, compared with 7 pounds or less for other species). This gives them commercial value and they are also coveted by sportsmen for their fight.

Pinks, the smallest and most numerous salmon statewide, will take a lure but are not widely sought by anglers because their flesh softens rapidly in fresh water. Natives utilize all species of salmon for commerical and subsistence use, and collect prize spawned-out salmon (*noodlevi*) which, though highly unattractive to sportsmen, are thought to be more digestible than salmon which have not spawned.

Less attention has been paid to the

*Clockwise from right*—A big grayling caught in the Bristol Bay region. / Cutthroat trout taken in one of the area's rivers. / A nice pike, caught near King Salmon. / A hefty arctic char. (All photos by Lou Gwartney)

An arctic grayling (top) and two rainbow trout caught in the Wood River Lakes system. (Don Rogers, U.W. Fisheries Research Institute)

cohos, or silver salmon, although they provide an important late fishing season for villages like Port Heiden.

Sport fishing in the Bay area affords astonishing variety and large catches in almost every category. Ten-pound rainbow trout, arctic grayling in excess of three pounds, and super pike and Dolly Varden are not unusual; there are also whitefish, lake trout, arctic char, candlefish, burbot and others in these waters.

Bristol Bay is free of reptiles—as is most of the rest of Alaska—but boasts one amphibian, the wood frog (*rana sylvatica cantabrigenis*), which is considerably smaller than its proper name and favors the lake regions.

Balsam poplar near
Dumpling Mountain, in
Katmai National
Monument. Fireweed is
in the foreground in this
photo, taken in
September. (Nancy
Simmerman)

**B**ristol Bay's coastal plain features tundra bogs with willow and alder thickets along drainages up to an elevation of about 900 feet. This country is generally treeless except for small, scattered stands of spruce and balsam poplar. Shrubs include labrador tea, cassiope, mountain cranberry, bog blueberry, crowberry and bearberry. Flowers of infinite color and variety also nestle among tundra grasses.

In the interior, spruce and balsam poplar take over, bordering the reaches of the Mulchatna and Nushagak rivers. Sizable areas of resin birch and willows, three to six feet tall, grow in the Iliamna Lake and Lake Clark area, and extend to the base of the Chigmit Mountains. Willow thickets and occasional outcroppings of alder are common along the lakes, streams and flood plains.

Upland white spruce are 40 to 80 feet high and 8 to 16 inches in diameter; there are also some black spruce and mountain hemlock, as well as white birch and aspen on burned-out slopes. Thick forests of

Lake Clark, third largest in the Bristol Bay region, has been called one of the most beautiful bodies of water in the world. (Reprinted from *ALASKA* ® magazine)

100-year-old spruce are found in the Aleknagik River area and to the east is a dense forest of Sitka and white spruce.

Of some 2,741,000 acres of forest, only 704,000 acres in the northern area of the region are estimated to have commercial potential, but value to Bristol Bay wildlife should not be underestimated.

# Historically, the Bay has been subject to the whims of Outside ownership

Mrs. Simeon Bartman of Manokotak village cleans salmon and sheefish, setting aside pinkish-orange skeins of salmon roe. Stocks of salmon appear healthy in the region, but subsistence hunting and trapping have been threatened. Moose and caribou numbers are down, and other species have reportedly dropped off in recent years.

# Wealth and Economy

As in aboriginal times, the economy of Bristol Bay today is based on the sea—primarily the salmon industry and the boom/bust cycles that go with it.

From 1961 to 1972 the average wholesale value of the catch was $30 million. In 1970 it netted $27 million. In 1974, the year the Bay was declared a disaster area and experienced the second worst catch in its 82-year history—the worst being 1973—the total was only $6 million. In 1977 the product was valued at about $32 million, a definite improvement.

The Bristol Bay Regional Development Council, established in 1974 to broaden economic options, realized from the outset its task was not simple.

"It would be naive to suggest that the economic, cultural and social structure of Bristol Bay region will not continue to be intrinsically interwoven around the

fishing industry in the foreseeable future," the council allowed in an early publication. "The approach in this report will be to find ways to magnify the economic opportunities surrounding the fishing industry."

Happily, biologists' forecasts for the next five years are optimistic, although reasons for the larger 1977 run have not been pinpointed. It could be that the scientific tools of management are better honed than in years past, and perhaps

Spawning sockeye salmon in Hansen Creek, near Lake Aleknagik. Runs have been larger in recent years, mostly due to improved management techniques. (Dan Moriarity, U. W. Fisheries Research Institute)

*Clockwise from above* — A Native woman cleans sockeye salmon for drying. / The former *Star of Alaska,* an iron-hulled square-rigger once owned by the Alaska Packers Association, often sailed to Bristol Bay for loads of salmon. The ship now bears her original name, *Balclutha,* and is berthed in San Francisco. / J. Scott Carter, right, and fishing partner Carl Alto aboard a gill-net boat in the Naknek-Kvichak district of Bristol Bay. (All photos by J. Scott Carter, reprinted from *ALASKA* ® magazine)

limited entry and the recently imposed 200-mile limit on foreign fishermen have had an effect. (Or it could be a fluke and the future may not be as bright as expected.) The really good news, in any case, is that financial gains from the fishery—even in poor years—are going more into local pockets.

**H**istorically, the Bay has been subject to the whims of Outside ownership—the old company store syndrome—with most of the money generated there going out of state in payment to nonresidents. And, although the majority of the Bay's 22 processing plants and several floating operations are still held by Outsiders (particularly the Japanese), local control is growing.

In 1973 a local fisherman's co-op was formed to develop cold-storage operations, and failed the same year. However, the Tonuak Indian Credit Association has helped a number of local men finance their own boats and break away from cannery-owned fleets.

An old double-ended Bristol Bay sailboat, symbol of earlier days, sails along after being salvaged from one of the Bay's canneries. The new owner of this boat was lucky—most of the sailboats are gone and it would now be difficult to assemble one complete, "original" model including sails and rigging. (Dean Kendall, reprinted from *ALASKA* ® magazine)

73

In 1973 the city of Dillingham built a $1.24 million cold-storage plant with dock facilities which, despite engineering problems and a few bumpy years, has successfully competed with the cannery that formerly monopolized business there. This, along with other factors, has helped increase prices paid to local fishermen.

Then, in 1976, Bristol Bay Native Corporation bought out Peter Pan Seafoods, one of the area's largest processers, reorganized the troubled company and reportedly earned back much of the purchase price ($9 million) in the first few years of operation.

A number of Bay village corporations have also invested money in fishing ventures and, although they have problems competing with their parent regional, their enterprise may yet fill local coffers.

Then there is limited entry, a hotly debated state law that restricts Bay fishing to those with a permit. Many outsiders are allowed to participate

*Continued on page 79*

A member of the beach gang uses a fire hose to force a scow full of Bristol Bay sockeye salmon onto a loading conveyor. (J. Scott Carter, reprinted from *ALASKA* ® magazine)

74

# ... TOWARD COMPUTERIZED FISHERIES MANAGEMENT IN BRISTOL BAY

By Dr. Ole A. Mathisen
UNIVERSITY OF WASHINGTON
FISHERIES RESEARCH INSTITUTE

**A**n important factor in the Bristol Bay fishery has been the strong tides, and compared with other regions, the tides have made traps, purse seines or beach seines at river mouths inefficient. After some limited use, the traps and seines were abandoned in favor of gill nets. Initially the mesh sizes were large, up to 6 inches, and since male salmon are larger than females, the size-selective gill nets caught predominantly males—as much as 80% of the catch—which yielded the best pack. The result was that, in spite of heavy fishing pressure, a sufficient number of females escaped during the early years of exploitation to ensure a proper egg deposition. (Subsequent research has demonstrated that all eggs will be fertilized despite a surplus of females on the spawning grounds.)

However, after 30 years of fishing, the Bristol Bay stocks experienced a decline. In the Nushagak the average catch fell suddenly from five million fish to three million. There were several contributing reasons. The mesh sizes commonly used decreased from 6¼ inches to 5¾ inches and even to 5½ inches, with the result that the potential egg deposition fell with the increased removal of females by the smaller nets. The biogenic elements brought into the lake system and nursery areas from the decaying salmon carcasses reduced primary and secondary production, and thereby, the food for the juvenile sockeye salmon in the nursery area.

From 1920 to the end of the Second World War, the Bristol Bay fishery continued at a lower production level. Although catches for the total Bay remained high until the late 1930's, smaller districts like the Ugashik quickly succumbed to heavy fishing pressure. The Nushagak continued fairly well, perhaps partly because of an intensive predator control in the 1930's. The Kvichak cycle showed increased oscillations with peak catches occurring during the 1930's, followed by very low ones. This overall decline and the violent fluctuations in the Kvichak system raised grave concern for proper management and conservation procedures in some districts.

The first steps were taken even before the turn of the century—remedial actions which aimed at making the fishing gear less efficient by removing fishing operations from the river mouths, by controlling the entire fishing season and by closing the fishery for certain periods. A quantum step was made in 1924 with passage of the White Act, prescribing a 50-50 division of the run into catch and escapement. (In retrospect, a fishing mortality of 50% is not far from the one being maintained today on many occasions.) But, the important fact is that for the first time size of the escapement was prescribed as a prerequisite for a good management system.

Unfortunately, this goal was not realized, simply because

*Plankton samples are taken at Lake Aleknagik, part of studies which have helped boost salmon production in recent years.* (U. W. Fisheries Research Institute)

*A biologist counts passing salmon from a tower at Ugashik Lake.* (Rick Furniss)

there was no way to accurately estimate the escapement. Weirs were tried, but they were costly, difficult to install and maintain, inefficient or even directly harmful. Ground surveys were completely inadequate.

Finally, the salmon industry took direct steps. In 1945 Dr. W. F. Thompson, who at that time was in charge of the University of Washington School of Fisheries, and also director of the Fraser River sockeye salmon investigations, was asked to study the salmon problems in Bristol Bay. This venture was unique: research money was given without directives to the university, and all information became public property. However, there was no managerial responsibility.

During the late 1940's and into the 1950's, research produced systems to sample the catch, measure escapement through visual tower counts, gauge smolt production by net catches, and assess juvenile sockeye salmon abundance in the nursery lakes by tow-net catches. The life history of sockeye salmon was divided into 11 stages where abundance could be monitored. Thus, a system of sequential forecasting was born, where observations on abundance and survival during one life stage would form the input for prediction of abundance in the next stage. Starting with the escapement, a forecast sequence can be made covering the fresh-water life of the salmon, followed by abundance estimates during the ocean residence, and finally, precise abundance estimates of the incoming mature fish before their entry into the fishery.

Two things plagued federal management authorities during the 1950's—the shift from sailing gill-netters to power-boats between 1951-1953, which increased the fishing power of a single boat, and the continuous increase in the number of boats in the fleet, caused in part by the influx of part-time fishermen.

Next, the introduction of nylon gill nets opened the way for the Japanese high-seas salmon fishery, which commenced in 1953 and quickly grew to a yearly landing of more than 20 million salmon of mixed origin. The peak harvest of salmon of Bristol Bay origin exceeded six million fish in 1956.

Over the years there has been a consistent drive to reduce or eliminate the Japanese high-seas fishery on sock-

*Greg Simmons, a researcher, removes a male sockeye from a beach seine at Little Togiak Lake. (Glen McDevitt)*

eye salmon stocks of Bristol Bay origin. Constraints have been imposed on the Japanese high-seas mothership fishery, but it took the introduction of a 200-mile fishing zone to achieve adequate protection from this fishery. This was largely possible because of the tagging studies and other biological investigations which had clearly defined the areas and the time periods when Bristol Bay sockeye salmon would be present.

Recently a Japanese land-based fishery has developed, expanding rapidly to exceed catches of the mothership fleet. There is a need to establish whether or not a significant number of Bristol Bay salmon are taken in this Japanese land-based high-seas fishery—if so, management authority could be extended to protect these anadromous species.

Other attempts were made in the 1950's to trim the harvest of salmon in Bristol Bay. An effort to cut efficiency of gear by a reduction timetable was tried, but escapement goals still had not been clearly formulated and the attempt failed. Eventually, with year-after-year samplings of

catch and escapement by the Fisheries Research Institute, escapement goals were formulated with a scientific basis and the first optimum escapement was established in 1957 for the Nushagak district.

With statehood in 1958, salmon management took another step forward. Management control was transferred to Bristol Bay allowing decisions to be made on a day-to-day basis to conform to incoming evidence. For the first time the emphasis shifted from deriving a so-called optimum sustainable catch to that of securing an optimum escapement. The gradually increasing trend of the Bristol Bay fishery has proved the wisdom of this decision. Some cold winters and late springs in 1971-1973 caused a temporary setback, but these damages were subsequently repaired by wise management of reduced returns.

Many other innovations have now sharpened the management process. Test fishing at the upper boundary of the commerical fishing zone produces an index of the escapement up to four to five days before the fish pass the tower counting stations. Test fishing at Port Moller, about

120 miles from inner Bristol Bay, provides another estimate of the total Bay run one week before the salmon reach the fishing districts.

All data collected during the postwar period were assembled in 1972 into a computerized data file that now has been transferred from the University of Washington to the University of Alaska, which has become the permanent repository. It is an open file, available to all people needing this information, keeping in part with the growing understanding that the balanced science management of renewable resources ultimately is a political decision, and the best decision requires an informed citizenry.

From a computerized data file, it is only a short step to a computerized management system with initial decisions based on average entry patterns. This works very well in Bristol Bay because of the short duration of the runs in the fishery.

In retrospect, the management system that has emerged for the sockeye salmon in Bristol Bay ranks as one of the best and most efficient and might well serve as a model elsewhere. □

*Clockwise from left*—Stacks of boxes tell the story— salmon roe bound for Japan from a Port Moller cannery. / Yoshi Atkashi, in a Port Moller cannery, prepares salmon-egg caviar for shipment to Japan. / Sockeye salmon are carried up a conveyor system to the processing line in a Dillingham cannery. (Toby Thaler)

78

simply because they fished the area in years past, and many local people are excluded—especially inland Natives who found it unprofitable to fish the Bay during poor fishing years, which later became the qualifying years. But, whether fishing pressure actually decreases or not, the system does put a stop to fishermen entering the area in ever-increasing numbers. The price of permits has risen astonishingly and some fear that soon only Outsiders will be able to afford them. It is conceivable, however, that well-heeled Native corporations will also compete, thus increasing local control.

Revitalization of the fishing industry comes at a time when other economic options loom. Most promising—or threatening, depending on your point of view—is development of offshore oil and gas fields, which could hold potential danger for Bristol Bay fish.

In 1977 the petroleum industry named Bristol Bay its number three target in the nation for offshore oil drilling and there's little doubt that an uncontrolled spill could seriously damage salmon stocks. The federal Outer Continental Shelf

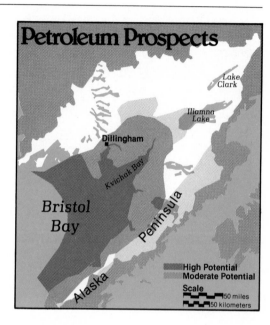

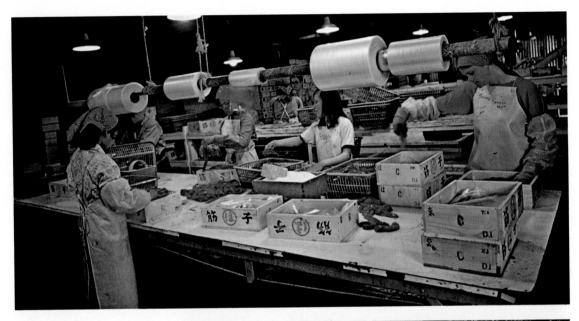

*Above*—Processing salmon roe for the Japanese market at Dillingham. (Neil and Betty Johannsen)
*Right*—Cans of salmon await shipment to market in a Bristol Bay plant. The industry is recovering from hard times in 1973 and 1974. (J. Scott Carter, reprinted from *ALASKA*® magazine)

agency was caught short by the offshore-drilling announcement for it had only begun to study possible environmental impacts on the area. The feeling is that industry will not be allowed to have its choice . . . at least not immediately. (Bristol Bay is potentially part of the Cook Inlet Mesozoic Province, where oil has already been discovered and developed, and may also prove an extension of rich fields now being tapped in Russia, which makes it a prime target in an energy crisis.)

The history of onshore exploration is not imposing. Early-day prospectors found several oil and gas seepages in 1902, but by 1957 only 12 wells had been completed. Results were apparently poor in each case. Two wells have since been drilled near Egegik, one south of Pilot Point, one near Ugashik, one offshore near Port Heiden to test state tidelands, and one near Ivanof Bay—all with discouraging results.

Exploration is definitely continuing, however, under the auspices of the Bristol Bay Native Corporation, a major landholder.

"Since there are no salmon and

continual unemployment, I feel if I could get some industry here other than fishing, I'd be doing my people a service," explained BBNC president Harvey Samuelson during the fishing crisis of 1974, and even though fishing prospects are considerably brighter today, his firm remains enthusiastic about petroleum.

"I've had letters of objection from many villages that are scared of the oil industry, but it's because they don't know anything about it. Fear it will clutter up the country," Samuelson reports. "But with modern technology, oil and a fishery can be compatible."

Pete Petta, Sr. and Jr., trapping partners from Kogliginak, display a stretched beaver pelt in front of their cabin.

The Bay area has long been thought to have other mineral potential—perhaps even greater than oil—but early miners will tell you this wealth is illusive.

At the turn of the century there was a modest rush of gold miners to the upper Mulchatna River and Lake Clark areas, but those who traveled that country to trap showed greater profit. Today there is

*Above*—Iliamna Lake, largest in Alaska with 1,000 square miles, can be just about as rough as the ocean when a storm arrives. This photograph, taken in March, illustrates the point—the barge is being tossed over huge swells like a bathtub toy. (Roland Moody) *Opposite*—Sunset at Lake Aleknagik on an unusually calm evening. (Brenda Rogers, U. W. Fisheries Research Institute)

one working gold mine north of Lake Clark, apparently not a bonanza.

More promising, perhaps, is a huge low-grade copper deposit—the largest copper claim in the state—on the as-yet-undeveloped shores of Kontrashibuna Lake. While the claim is held by the influential Guggenheim family, the site lies within lands identified under Section (d)-2 of the Alaska Native Claims Settlement Act, and is coveted by the federal government as a potential wilderness area. Copper mining will probably not come to Kontrashibuna.

Coal deposits have been found in the Chigmit Mountains and off Port Moller. Uranium is definitely suspected, but even if deposits prove sizable, problems of

transport are expected to stop developers for years to come.

The same is true with the harvest of timber wealth . . . which the region definitely possesses. Pile Bay, for example, got its name because 19th century salmon packers cut some pilings for their canneries and mammoth docks from this area . . . then floated them to destinations throughout the region. However, it would be difficult to ship Bay lumber to Outside markets for want of a deepwater port, and regrowth in the region is slow.

Farming potential is good in permafrost-free areas. A larger local market makes truck gardening more feasible than in years past, but the

*Continued on page 87*

# AIR SERVICE TO BRISTOL BAY

By Jim Dodson Jr.
ALASKA AIR CARRIERS
ASSOCIATION

Airplane service to the Bristol Bay area didn't start at the same time Noel Wien and Roy Jones were barnstorming their way into the Interior and Southeastern Alaska, but when the first plane did make it through the mountain passes from Cook Inlet, air travel caught on just as quickly as it had elsewhere—maybe faster, because by the early 1930's the equipment was a lot more dependable and capable than Wien's Hisso-Standard J-1 or Jones's MF Flying Boat, the *Northbird*.

Stinsons, Travel Air 6000's, Fairchild 71's and Bellancas were the ships of the 30's and they could carry a decent load at a fairly respectable altitude, far enough to make travel by air to Bristol Bay realistic.

Mail boosted air service in the region, as elsewhere in Alaska, with early pilots following the dog sled trails, and making stops along the way to deliver the mail (under

contract to the U.S. Postal Department).

Salmon, however, were the reason air service could thrive. While other parts of Alaska had trapping and mining, Bristol Bay was, and still is, the home of the largest sockeye salmon spawning grounds in the world, and thousands came in the summer to take the harvest.

It was a long trip by sail or steam from the West Coast, across the Gulf of Alaska, around the Alaska Peninsula and up into the Bay. It was much faster and easier to fly, once airplanes were available and able to make the trip, and there were pilots able and investors willing.

So air routes were marked from Anchorage's Merrill Field, down the Kuskokwim to Bethel and over; and even across from Kodiak Island on a clear day.

In the summer, travel between the communities— usually between one cannery and another—constituted the commerce and pilots and planes began to stay in the communities. By the late 30's,

*Planes have been a major factor in Bristol Bay transportation since the 1930's. In this case, a chartered amphibian brings kayak-campers to the Tikchik Lakes region.*
(Neil and Betty Johannsen)

both Naknek and Dillingham had aircraft available most of the year and the year-round population began traveling, no longer by long, hard overland means, but through the air.

Bristol Bay abounds with lakes, streams and rivers. Every settlement was on water and the airplanes of the 30's and early 40's all used floats.

With the coming of the Second World War, air travel was advanced. The late 30's and early 40's had already

brought regular air service by Star, Woodly, McGee and Bowman between Anchorage and Naknek-Dillingham, and now, with the need for defense, came the military base at King Salmon, the DC-3's and other large transports, plus navigational aids and communication. Nothing advanced air travel in Alaska like the introduction of communication and navigational facilities. The military needs boosted air service out of the

*Left*—Supplies come to Bristol Bay primarily by barge and aircraft. Everyone pitches in when the barge arrives at Aleknagik in June. (Don Rogers, U.W. Fisheries Research Institute)

*Clockwise from above*—An aerial view of Tikchik Narrows Lodge, in the rich Wood River-Tikchik Lakes region. Several lodges in the area appeal to fly-in fishermen, many from the Anchorage area. / Early spring is a time for festivals and dog races in several Bristol Bay towns and villages. Biggest of them all is the Beaver Roundup, held each February in Dillingham. (James Faro, reprinted from *The MILEPOST®*) / Margaret Clark and cook Carl Schoeller at Kvichak Lodge, Igiugig.

potential. There is a handsome new hotel at Dillingham, and Herman Herrmann's one-room hotel at Igiugig should not be underestimated.

Iliaska Lodge at Iliamna once concentrated only on sport fishermen but under new ownership has attracted a surprising number of nonfishermen—mostly camera fans and hikers. (Nearby Iliamna Lodge burned to the ground in the fall of 1977.)

Winter sports nuts, too, are finding Bristol Bay an exciting stop. There are carnivals, and snow machine and dog sled races are held during spring months at different villages around the Bay and up at the lake villages and the competition is keen.

Not to be overlooked, although mostly outside the strict boundaries of our geographic coverage, is Katmai National Monument, 4,200 square miles of volcanic crater lakes, glacier-covered peaks, ocean bays, fjords, wilderness forests and lagoons—reached almost exclusively by aircraft.

Doug Popham cross-country skis up Quartz Creek, in the Wood River drainage, with his Siberian husky pulling an 80-pound sled load. (Rollie Ostermick)

Gateway to the monument is King Salmon (contact the monument headquarters office in town for details).

Katmai, one of the largest preserves in the National Park system, was established in 1918 to set aside leftovers from what may have been the second-greatest volcanic eruption in recorded history. On June 1, 1912, the area surrounding Mount Katmai experienced a series of tremors. These grew in intensity until on June 6, at the present site of Novarupta Volcano, halfway between the then-existing villages of Katmai and Savonoski, a thunderous blast spewed forth masses of

The Valley of Ten Thousand Smokes is distinguished by rhyolite cliffs cut from ash deposits along the Ukak River. Some of the cliffs are 100 feet high. (Nancy Simmerman)

pumice and rock. Within minutes, 2.5 cubic miles of ash were ejected and swept down adjacent valleys. More than 40 square miles of the Katmai area—today called the Valley of Ten Thousand Smokes—was buried to depths as great as 700 feet.

At about the same time Novarupta was belching forth pumice and ash, the top of Mount Katmai volcano, 6 miles to the east, collapsed, creating a huge chasm. During the period after Novarupta's eruption, 7 cubic miles of volcanic material were hurled into the atmosphere and carried by winds to all parts of the Northern Hemisphere. (For details on the Katmai eruption and other volcanic activity in Alaska, order *Alaska's Volcanoes: Northern Link in the Ring of Fire*. Please see page 96.)

Like many other parts of the Bristol Bay region, Katmai offers wilderness, wildlife and good fishing—the monument is world famous for its rainbow, salmon and grayling fishing. (For details, contact Park Superintendent, Katmai National Monument, P.O. Box 7, King Salmon, Alaska 99613.) Visitors may stay at Brooks River Lodge, on the Brooks River between Naknek and Brooks lakes; at fishing camps in the area, or at a free tent campground on the shore of Naknek Lake, near the lodge. Tours are arranged by the park concessionaire, Wien Air Alaska.

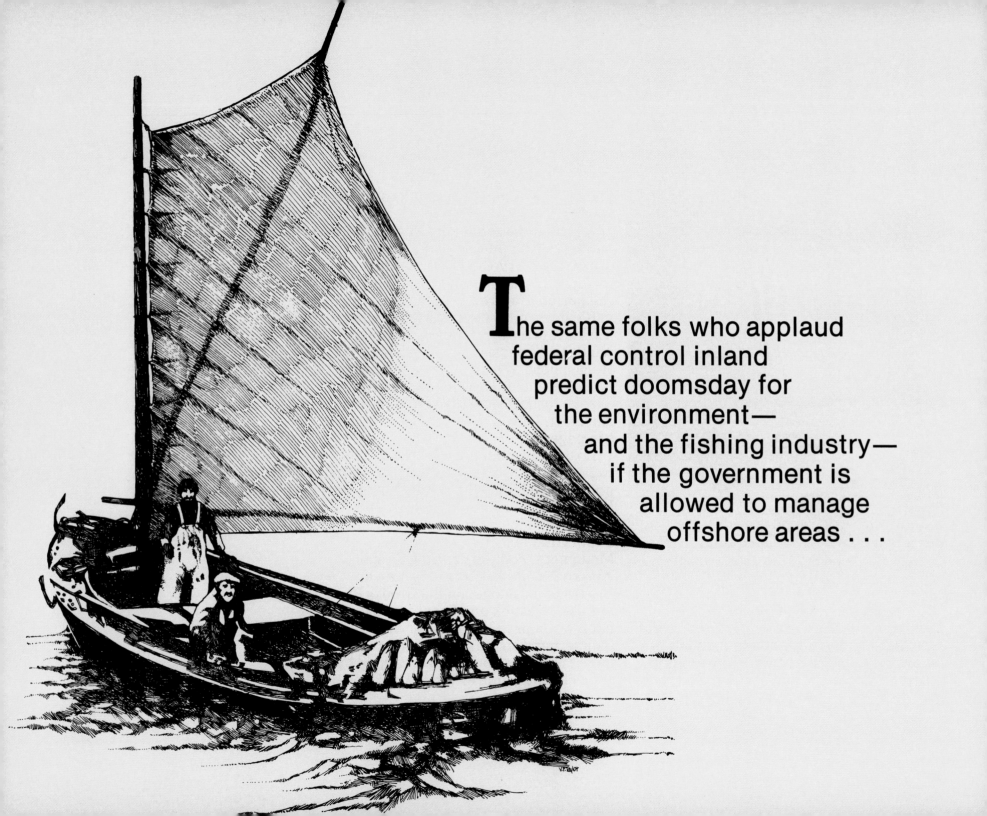

The same folks who applaud
federal control inland
predict doomsday for
the environment—
and the fishing industry—
if the government is
allowed to manage
offshore areas . . .

# The Future

Lake Clark homesteader Floyd Dennison recalls that until fairly recently the only land title readily considered in the Bristol Bay area was "squatter's rights."

"You owned your cabin and you owned your stove and that was about it. Old-timers used to get $30 a month from the territory if they'd signed papers saying the government was supposed to get their cabin and possessions when they died, but as far as I know it just never happened."

If disaster or epidemic hit, survivors picked another spot and settled without paperwork or second thought. Akulivikchuk, the largest and most important village on the Nushagak, took itself off the map in the late 1800's and residents dispersed in several directions after their children were lost when rotten river ice on which they were playing gave way.

When old Savonoski was destroyed by the Katmai eruptions in 1912, refugees created a new village on the south bank of the Naknek River, then abandoned it to search individually for new opportunity.

Families at Ilnik on the peninsula moved temporarily to Ugashik and then Port Heiden in pursuit of schooling for their youngsters and never got around to returning home. Although they'd left their Ilnik houses furnished and ready, the grass proved greener elsewhere. Open country offered promise—but no more.

Take a map of Bristol Bay and flap down an overlay showing lands in private ownership—just a dot here and there. Now add another overlay showing lands claimed by Native corporations; a third for land sought by the state, a fourth indicating parks and preserves sought by the federal government; a fifth showing projected roads and right-of-way corridors, and suddenly there's not

enough open country left to nest a ground squirrel. Presto! A glimpse into the future of the Bristol Bay region—the disappearance of wide-open country and, perhaps simultaneously, the erosion of lifestyles that cannot exist with rules and amenities.

It's not a question of whether or not the land will be parceled off, but how and when. Who will get what? If conservationists win (and this is a simplified view, to be sure), mineral development and land promotion could be stymied. While much acreage is in the hands of Native corporations, they are committed by law to profit-making ventures for their stockholders. The federal government is pressing for wilderness inland, but at the same time is under pressure from the petroleum industry to lease the Bay's outer continental shelf for oil exploration . . . and the same folks who applaud federal control inland predict doomsday for the environment—and the fishing industry—if the government is allowed to manage offshore areas.

The debates rage on—with merits to be weighed by Congress and perhaps also the federal courts. To date, input from Bay residents has had little bearing on the real issues. And historically, that figures . . . for "Outside control" has long been the price Bay folks have paid to occupy such valuable territory.

Togiak village overlooks Togiak Bay on the north side of Bristol Bay. On the horizon is High Island, in the Walrus Islands group. (Steve Westfall)

# Alaska Geographic. Back Issues

Single copies of the *ALASKA GEOGRAPHIC*® back issues are also available. When ordering, please add $.50 postage/handling per copy. Washington residents add 5.4% sales tax.

**The North Slope, Vol. 1, No. 1.** Charter issue of *ALASKA GEOGRAPHIC*®. Out of print.

**One Man's Wilderness, Vol. 1, No. 2.** The story of a dream shared by many, fulfilled by few: a man in our own time goes into the bush, builds a cabin and lives there 16 months. An incredible wilderness experience. Color photos. 116 pages, $7.95

**Admiralty . . . Island in Contention, Vol. 1, No. 3.** An intimate and multifaceted view of Admiralty: its geological and historical past, its present-day geography, wildlife and sparse human population. Discusses the views of factions "in contention" for the island. Color photos. 78 pages, $5.00

**Fisheries of the North Pacific: History, Species, Gear & Processes, Vol. 1, No. 4.** An excerpt from the book of the same title, this is a comprehensive source of information on commercial fishing in the waters from Baja California to the Aleutian Islands and the Bering Sea. 98 black-and-white and color photos. 123 pages, $7.95

**The Alaska-Yukon Wild Flowers Guide, Vol. 2, No. 1.** First Northland flower book with both large, color photos and detailed drawings of every species described. Features 160 species from every geographic area of Alaska and the Yukon. Common and scientific names, plus maximum growing height. 112 pages, $7.95

**Richard Harrington's Yukon, Vol. 2, No. 2.** A collection of 277 stunning color photos by Canadian photographer-writer Richard Harrington captures the Yukon in all its seasons and moods, from Watson Lake to Herschel Island. 103 pages, $7.95

**Prince William Sound, Vol. 2, No. 3.** Out of print.

**Yakutat: The Turbulent Crescent, Vol. 2, No. 4.** Yakutat, mystery area to travelers and Alaska residents, is now the major harbor for the fledgling Gulf of Alaska offshore oil industry. The story of a part of Alaska constantly changed by nature but little changed, so far, by man. Color photos. 81 pages, $7.95

**Glacier Bay: Old Ice, New Land, Vol. 3, No. 1.** The expansive wilderness of Southeastern Alaska's Glacier Bay National Monument unfolds in crisp text and color photographs. Records the flora and fauna of the area, its natural history, hike and cruise information for visitors. Glossary of plants and animals, large-scale color map included. 132 pages, $9.95

**The Land: Eye of the Storm, Vol. 3, No. 2.** Focuses on Alaska as "real estate." It is an effort to state fairly some of the key issues of the present that will have impact on the future. Clear, closely researched text sets forth the issues while fascinating full-color photographs bring the land in contention into visual focus. Color maps. 64 pages, $6.95

**Richard Harrington's Antarctic, Vol. 3, No. 3.** The Canadian photo-journalist guides armchair travelers/explorers/naturalists through the past and the present of the remote and little understood regions of the Antarctic and Subantarctic. More than 200 color photos and a very personal account. Separate map. 104 pages, $8.95

**The Silver Years of the Alaska Canned Salmon Industry: An Album of Historical Photos, Vol. 3, No. 4.** Commemorates a boom or bust era in Alaska's romantic history, and more than 293 photos record the history of the industry — late 19th century to the present. Sparse text links the photographs by subject — plants, boats and gear, transportation. 168 pages, $7.95

**Alaska's Volcanoes: Northern Link in the Ring of Fire, Vol. 4, No. 1.** Scientific overview supplemented with eyewitness accounts of some of North America's most violent eruptions: maps locate all of Alaska's historic volcano eruptions. Color and black-and-white photos and a schematic description of the effects of plate movement upon volcanic activity. 88 pages, $7.95

**The Brooks Range: Environmental Watershed, Vol. 4, No. 2.** Looks at early exploration by white men through journals, at historic periods that rival present interest in the area's natural wealth, and at controversy over uses for it: Native land claims, recreation, proposed national parks and development of resources. Maps, color photos. 112 pages, $9.95

**Kodiak: Island of Change, Vol. 4, No. 3.** Although half the size of New Jersey, and once the administrative center of Russian Alaska, the 3,588-square-mile island of Kodiak remains well off the beaten path. Past, present and future — everything from Russian exploration to the present-day quest for oil. Maps, color photos. 96 pages, $7.95

**Wilderness Proposals: Which Way for Alaska's Lands?, Vol. 4, No. 4.** Out of print.

**Cook Inlet Country, Vol. 5, No. 1.** A very special tour of the Cook Inlet region — its communities, big and small, and its countryside. Begins at the southern tip of the Kenai Peninsula, circles Turnagain Arm and Knik Arm for a close-up view of Anchorage, and visits the Matanuska and Susitna valleys and the wild, west side of the inlet. 144 pages; 230 color photos, separate map. $9.95

**Southeast: Alaska's Panhandle, Vol. 5, No. 2.** Most colorful edition to date, exploring Southeastern Alaska's maze of fjords and islands, mossy forests and glacier-draped mountains — from Dixon Entrance to Icy Bay, including all of the state's fabled Inside Passage. Along the way are profiles of every town, together with a look at the region's history, economy, people, attractions and future. Includes large fold-out map and seven area maps. 192 pages, $9.95

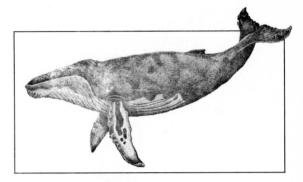

**COMING ATTRACTION**
**Alaska Whales and Whaling, Vol. 5, No. 4.** The wonders of whales in Alaska — their life cycles, travels and travails — are examined, along with an authoritative history of commercial and subsistence whaling in the North . . . with special focus on the issue of Eskimo bowhead whaling. Included are color photos and illustrations of 15 whales found in Alaskan waters, together with maps showing whale distribution. Introduction by Dr. Victor Scheffer, author of *Year of the Whale*. Mailed to members in September 1978. Price to be announced.

Your $20 initial membership in The Alaska Geographic Society includes 4 subsequent issues of *ALASKA GEOGRAPHIC*®, the Society's official quarterly. Renewals are $16. Please add $1 for non-U.S. membership.

Additional membership information available upon request. To order back issues send your check or money order and volumes desired to:

*The Alaska Geographic Society*

Box 4-EEE, Dept. AGS, Anchorage, AK 99509